Lecture Notes in Computer Science 12887

More information about this subseries at http://www.springer.com/series/7409

Jonathan Bright · Anastasia Giachanou ·
Viktoria Spaiser · Francesca Spezzano ·
Anna George · Alexandra Pavliuc (Eds.)

Disinformation in Open Online Media

Third Multidisciplinary International Symposium, MISDOOM 2021
Virtual Event, September 21–22, 2021
Proceedings

 Springer

Editors
Jonathan Bright
University of Oxford
Oxford, UK

Anastasia Giachanou
Utrecht University
Utrecht, The Netherlands

Viktoria Spaiser (iD)
University of Leeds
Leeds, UK

Francesca Spezzano
Boise State University
Boise, ID, USA

Anna George
University of Oxford
Oxford, UK

Alexandra Pavliuc
University of Oxford
Oxford, UK

ISSN 0302-9743   ISSN 1611-3349   (electronic)
Lecture Notes in Computer Science
ISBN 978-3-030-87030-0   ISBN 978-3-030-87031-7   (eBook)
https://doi.org/10.1007/978-3-030-87031-7

LNCS Sublibrary: SL3 – Information Systems and Applications, incl. Internet/Web, and HCI

This Springer imprint is published by the registered company Springer Nature Switzerland AG
The registered company address is: Gewerbestrasse 11, 6330 Cham, Switzerland

Preface

Online media have become a politically, economically, and organizationally critical infrastructure. Internet users all over the world can directly interact with each other and participate in political discussions. Through online media, journalists have access to enormous amounts of information and public sentiment that increasingly becomes part of their reporting. Politicians refine their positions and actions based on the (seemingly) public opinion, which they distill from online media. Others use these channels to distribute their views. Companies allow product reviews by users to provide crowd-based quality assurance. The Multidisciplinary International Symposium on Disinformation in Open Online Media (MISDOOM) brings together researchers from multiple disciplines, including communication science, computer science, computational social science, political communication, journalism, and media studies, as well as practitioners in journalism and online media. The symposium has a strong multidisciplinary character and aims to cater to the habits of different disciplines.

This volume contains the papers accepted to the Third Multidisciplinary International Symposium on Disinformation in Open Online Media (MISDOOM 2021). This volume also includes the abstracts of the talks given by the three invited keynote speakers. In light of the COVID-19 pandemic, the symposium took place during September 21–22, 2021, in a fully virtual format. In total, there were 100 submissions

Fig. 1. Topics of MISDOOM 2021. Size is proportional to the frequency of the word in the titles of the submissions accepted to the symposium.

(after desk rejections): 27 full papers and 73 extended abstracts. The Organizing Committee decided to accept 9 full paper submissions in the computer science track for publication in this LNCS volume. In addition, 75 contributions (full paper and abstract submissions) were accepted for presentation at the symposium. Among them, some submissions were considered for publication in a special issue of the *Social Media + Society* journal. Figure 1 shows a summary of the topics of all contributions to the symposium.

We want to express our gratitude towards all those who contributed to organizing and running this symposium. This includes the Program Committee, the local organizers, last year's organizing committee, the University of Oxford, the Oxford Internet Institute, and Green Templeton College at the University of Oxford. We hope that participants of all communities taking part in this multidisciplinary endeavor had a nice symposium and found some new insights and personal connections, especially between communities that usually do not meet so often in a symposium setting.

September 2021

Jonathan Bright
Anastasia Giachanou
Viktoria Spaiser
Francesca Spezzano
Anna George
Alexandra Pavliuc

Organization

General Chairs

Jonathan Bright   Oxford Internet Institute, UK
Anastasia Giachanou   Universiteit Utrecht, Netherlands

Program Committee Chairs

Viktoria Spaiser   University of Leeds, UK
Francesca Spezzano   Boise State University, USA

Outreach Chair

Anna George   Oxford Internet Institute, UK

Communications Chair

Alexandra Pavliuc   Oxford Internet Institute, UK

Program Committee

Meysam Alizadeh	Princeton University, USA
Kelechi Amakoh	Aarhus University, Denmark
Adriana Amaral	Unisinos, Brazil
Dennis Assenmacher	University of Münster, Germany
Ebrahim Bagheri	Ryerson University, Canada
Giulio Barbero	University of Leiden, Netherlands
Cody Buntain	New York University, USA
Christian Burgers	Vrije Universiteit Amsterdam, Netherlands
André Calero Valdez	RWTH Aachen University, Germany
Chico Camargo	University of Exeter, UK
Tommaso Caselli	Rijksuniversiteit Groningen, Netherlands
Travis Coan	University of Exeter, UK
Nicoleta Corbu	National University of Political Studies and Public Administration, Romania
Stefano Cresci	IIT-CNR, Italy
Anne Dirskon	University of Leiden, Netherlands
Mona Elswah	Oxford Internet Institute, UK
Eric Fernandes de Mello Araujo	Vrije Universiteit Amsterdam, Netherlands
Lena Frischlich	University of Münster, Germany
Matteo Gagliolo	Université libre de Bruxelles, Belgium

Łukasz Gajewski	Warsaw University of Technology, Poland
Ansgard Heinrich	University of Groningen, Netherlands
Aliaksandr Herasimenka	Oxford Internet Institute, UK
Hendrik Heuer	University of Bremen, Germany
Neta Kligler Vilenchik	Hebrew University of Jerusalem, Israel
Aleksi Knuutila	Oxford Internet Institute, UK
Elena Kochkina	Queen Mary University, UK
Elly Konijn	Vrije Universiteit Amsterdam, Netherlands
Dennis M. Riehle	Universität Koblenz-Landau, Germany
Sílvia Majó-Vázquez	University of Oxford, UK
Mehwish Nasim	CSIRO Data61, Australia
German Neubaum	University of Duisburg-Essen, Germany
Tom Nicholls	University of Oxford, UK
Marco Niemann	University of Münster, Germany
Henna Paakki	Aalto University, Finland
Maziyar Panahi	Institut des Systèmes Complexes Paris Île-de-France, France
Myrto Pantazi	Oxford Internet Institute, UK
Thorsten Quandt	University of Münster, Germany
Raquel Recuero	Universidade Federal de Pelotas, Brazil
Jan Schacht	HAW Hamburg, Germany
Tim Schatto-Eckrodt	University of Münster, Germany
Marcel Schliebs	Oxford Internet Institute, UK
Alon Sela	Ariel University, Israel
Louis Shekhtman	Bar Ilan University, Israel
Ross Towns	University of Leiden, Netherlands
Heike Trautmann	University of Münster, Germany
Marina Tulin	Erasmus University Rotterdam, Netherlands
Milos Ulman	Czech University of Life Sciences, Czechia
Peter van der Putten	University of Leiden and Pegasystems, Netherlands
Heidi Vepsäläinen	University of Helsinki, Finland
Gerhard Weiss	Maastricht University, Netherlands
Martin Wettstein	University of Zurich, Switzerland
Florian Wintterlin	University of Münster, Germany
Taha Yasseri	University College Dublin, Ireland
Arkaitz Zubiaga	Queen Mary University, UK

Keynotes

Russian Disinformation, Five Years Later

Nina Jankowicz

Global Fellow, Wilson Center
Nina.Jankowicz@wilsoncenter.org

Abstract. Since revelations of Russian online influence campaign first broke in 2016, the United States and the Western world has finally begun to wake up to the threat of online warfare and the attacks from Russia. The question no one seems to be able to answer is: what can the West do about it? Central and Eastern European states, however, have been aware of the threat for years. Nina Jankowicz has advised these governments on the front lines of the information war. In her keynote speech at MISDOOM, she will explore the threat of state-backed online disinformation, how it has changed since it became a blockbuster news story, and government responses to the phenomenon over the past five years.

Biography

Nina Jankowicz is an internationally-recognized expert on disinformation and democratization. Her debut book, *How to Lose the Information War* [6] (Bloomsbury/IBTauris), was named a *New Statesman* 2020 book of the year [1]; *The New Yorker* called it "a persuasive new book on disinformation as a geopolitical strategy." [2] Her next book, *How to Be A Woman Online*, an examination of online abuse and disinformation and tips for fighting back, will be published by Bloomsbury in Spring 2022.

Jankowicz's expertise spans the public, private, and academic sectors. She has advised governments, international organizations, and tech companies; testified before the United States Congress and European Parliament; and led accessible, actionable research about the effects of disinformation on women, minorities, democratic activists, and freedom of expression around the world. Jankowicz has extensive media experience, with writing published in many major American newspapers and magazines, including *The New York Times* [3], *The Washington Post* [4], and *The Atlantic* [5]. She is a regular guest on major radio and television programs such as the PBS Newshour, CNN's Fareed Zakaria GPS and Amanpour, the BBC World Service, and NPR's All Things Considered. Since 2017, Jankowicz has held fellowships at the Wilson Center[1], where she has been affiliated with the Kennan Institute and the Science and Technology Innovation Program. In 2016–2017, she advised the Ukrainian Foreign Ministry on disinformation and strategic communications under the auspices of a Fulbright-Clinton Public Policy Fellowship. Prior to her Fulbright grant, she managed democracy assistance programs to Russia and Belarus at the National Democratic Institute.

Jankowicz holds a Master's degree from the Center for Eurasian, Russian, and East European Studies at Georgetown University's School of Foreign Service. She is a proud alumna of Bryn Mawr College, where she studied Political Science and Russian and graduated magna cum laude. She is fluent in Russian, and speaks proficient Ukrainian and Polish, and serves on the Board of Trustees for the Eurasia Foundation.

References

1. https://www.newstatesman.com/best-books-2020
2. https://www.newyorker.com/magazine/2020/09/14/is-russian-meddling-as-dangerous-as-we-think
3. https://www.nytimes.com/2017/09/25/opinion/the-only-way-to-defend-against-russias-information-war.html
4. https://www.washingtonpost.com/opinions/2021/03/25/threat-deepfakes-isnt-hypothetical-women-feel-it-every-day/
5 https://www.theatlantic.com/technology/archive/2020/10/how-coronavirus-denialist-celebrity-made/616486/
6 Jankowicz, N.: How to Lose the Information War: Russia, Fake News, and the Future of Conflict. Bloomsbury Publishing (2020)

---

[1] https://www.wilsoncenter.org/person/nina-jankowicz.

Psychological Inoculation Against Misinformation

Sander van der Linden

Department of Psychology, School of Biology, University of Cambridge, UK
sander.vanderlinden@psychol.cam.ac.uk

Abstract. Much like a viral contagion, false information can spread rapidly from one individual to another. Moreover, once lodged in memory, misinformation is difficult to correct. Inoculation theory therefore offers a natural basis for developing a psychological 'vaccine' against the spread of fake news and misinformation. Specifically, in a series of randomized lab and field studies, we show that it is possible to pre-emptively "immunize" people against disinformation about climate change, COVID-19, and elections (amongst other topics) by pre-exposing them to severely weakened doses of the techniques that underlie its production. This psychological process helps people cultivate cognitive antibodies in a simulated social media environment. During the talk, I'll showcase an award-winning real-world intervention ("*Bad News*") we developed and empirically evaluated in 20 languages—with governments and social media companies—to help citizens around the world recognize and resist unwanted attempts to influence and mislead.

Introduction

Much like a viral contagion, false information can spread rapidly from one individual to another. In fact, models from epidemiology are increasingly used to study the viral spread of misinformation in social networks. Unfortunately, once lodged in memory, misinformation is difficult to correct. People often continue to retrieve falsehoods from memory even when acknowledging a correction, a phenomenon known as the continued influence of misinformation. Inoculation theory therefore offers a natural basis for developing a psychological 'vaccine' against the spread of fake news and misinformation. The theory of psychological inoculation follows the biomedical immunization analogy: just as weakened doses of viral pathogens trigger the production of antibodies to help the body fight off future infection, the same can be achieved with information. By pre-emptively exposing people to severely weakened doses of misinformation or the strategies used in its production, people can build up cognitive antibodies against misinformation. Specifically, in a series of randomized lab and field studies, we show that it is possible to pre-emptively "immunize" people against disinformation about climate change, COVID-19, and elections (amongst other topics) by pre-exposing them to severely weakened doses of the techniques that underlie its production. This psychological process helps people cultivate cognitive antibodies in a simulated social media environment. I'll review several award-winning real-world interventions we developed and empirically evaluated in 20 languages—with governments and (social) media companies—to help citizens around the world recognize and resist unwanted attempts to influence and mislead. *Bad News* is a serious social impact game (Fig. 1) that exposes people to weakened doses of the strategies used to spread misinformation, including polarizing audiences, the use of negative emotions (e.g., fearmongering), conspiracy theories, and impersonating fake experts. In a large within-subject study with about 15,000 individuals we found that playing the game improves people's ability to spot fake social media content post-gameplay. In several pre-registered randomized controlled trials we further found that the game improves people's confidence in their own truth-discernment abilities and that the effects can last up to several months with regular "booster" sessions. We extend these results into the domain of COVID-19 with *GoViral!*, a 5-minute game developed with the UK Government (with support from the World Health Organization and the United Nations) and into the area of electoral disinformation with *Harmony Square*, a similar game designed with CISA and the U.S. Department of Homeland Security. We are currently working on agent-based models to explore the potential for psychological herd immunity in online social networks.

Fig. 1. Bad News (www.getbadnews.com), Harmony Square (www.harmonysquare.game), and Go Viral! (www.goviralgame.com) game environments. Credit: DROG and Design Agency Gusmanson (reprinted with permission).

Biography

Sander van der Linden, Ph.D., is Professor of Social Psychology in Society and Director of the Cambridge Social Decision-Making Lab in the Department of Psychology at the University of Cambridge. He has won numerous awards for his research on human judgment, communication, and decision-making, including the Rising Star Award from the Association for Psychological Science (APS), the Sage Early Career Award from the Society for Personality and Social Psychology (SPSP), the Frank Prize in Public Interest Research from the

University of Florida and the Sir James Cameron Medal for the Public Understanding of Risk from the Royal College of Physicians.

He co-designed the award-winning fake news game Bad News, which has been played by millions of people around the world and frequently advises governments and social media companies on how to fight misinformation. His research is regularly featured in outlets such as the New York Times, NPR, Rolling Stone, and the BBC and he has been described by WIRED magazine as one of "15 top thinkers" and by Fast Company Design as one "four heroes who are defending digital democracy online". He is currently working on two new books "The Truth Vaccine" (WW Norton/HarperCollins) and the Psychology of Misinformation (Cambridge University Press). Before joining Cambridge, he held academic positions at Princeton, Yale, and the LSE.

Computational Challenges and Recent Advancements in Automated Fake News Detection

Reza Zafarani

Data Lab, Department of Electrical Engineering and Computer Science,
Syracuse University
reza@data.syr.edu

Abstract. "Fake news" is now viewed as one of the greatest threats to democracy, freedom of expression, and journalism. Massive spread of fake news has weakened public trust in governments and its potential impact on various political processes, e.g., the "Brexit" referendum or the equally divisive 2016 U. S. presidential election, is yet to be realized. We will briefly review some of the modern computational techniques for fake news detection, along with some of the current challenges that these methods face. We will discuss some recent advancements to tackle these challenges, with particular focus on fake news early detection, multimodal fake news analysis, modeling the intent of fake news spreaders, and the lack of data.

Keywords: Fake news · Disinformation · Fake news detection

1 Introduction

Computational methods that detect fake news can be categorized into four main groups: (1) *Knowledge-based* methods, which detect fake news based on the false knowledge it carries; (2) *Style-based* methods, which analyze fake news writing style; (3) *propagation-based* methods, which look at the propagation patterns of news articles among users that are spreading it; and (4) *Source-based* methods, which analyze the credibility of the initiating source (e.g., a user or a news outlet) for fake news [9]. Such methods often face various computational challenges:

I. Fake News Early Detection. The objective of fake news early detection is to detect fake news at an early stage before it becomes widespread. This allows one to take early actions for fake news mitigation and intervention. Early detection of fake news is especially crucial as the more fake news spreads, the more likely for individuals to trust it (e.g., due to *validity effect* [1]). To detect fake news at an early stage, one has to primarily and efficiently rely on news content and limited information, leading to multiple challenges. For example, the limited information that exists on fake news in its early propagation stages may adversely impact the performance of machine learning methods that most computational techniques are based on. We will discuss a recent text-based technology that we have developed that only relies on limited textual information, yet achieves state-of-the-art performance in fake news detection [6].

II. Detection of Non-Textual and Non-traditional Fake News. Most fake news detection methods solely use text. While news articles often contain images, not many studies have aimed at detecting fake news by exploring news images [5]. Similarly, not many studies have looked at multimodal (e.g., text+images) data. There is a significant need for methods that can combine multiple sources of information for better detection of fake news. We will discuss SAFE [8], a first of its kind technology that detects fake news by looking at the similarity between text and images in the articles.

III. Modeling Intent in Fake News Spreaders. A frequently observed phenomenon in the spread of fake news is that individuals can spread fake news *unintentionally* without recognizing its falseness [2, 9]. Clearly, the intervention strategy for malicious users that spread fake news and normal users that do the same should be different; malicious users should be penalized, while normal users should be assisted, e.g., by helping to improve their ability to distinguish fake news. For example, recommending articles with refuting evidence can be helpful to normal users. We will discuss some of our recent results on modelling the intention of fake news spreaders.

IV. Lack of Data. Most fake news detection techniques require historical data (i.e., *ground truth*) that contains fake and true news articles. Unfortunately, constructing such datasets often requires the help of domain experts that can act as fact-checkers to verify the authenticity of various news articles. Expert-based fact-checking is often conducted by a small group of highly credible fact-checkers and leads to highly accurate results. Unfortunately, the process is costly and poorly scales with the increase in the volume of the to-be-checked news contents; hence, it cannot be utilized to construct massive historical datasets that are often needed by computational techniques. We will discuss recent advancements and datasets, especially focusing on COVID-19 fake news, which aim to address this challenge [3, 4, 7].

References

1. Boehm, L.E.: The validity effect: a search for mediating variables. Pers. Soc. Psychol. Bull. **20** (3), 285–293 (1994)
2. Pennycook, G., Epstein, Z., Mosleh, M., Arechar, A.A., Eckles, D., Rand, D.G.: Shifting attention to accuracy can reduce misinformation online. Nature **592**(7855), 590–595 (2021)
3. Shu, K., Mahudeswaran, D., Wang, S., Lee, D., Liu, H.: FakeNewsNet: a data repository with news content, social context, and spatiotemporal information for studying fake news on social media. Big Data **8**(3), 171–188 (2020)
4. Yang, C., Zhou, X., Zafarani, R.: Checked: Chinese covid-19 fake news dataset. Soc. Netw. Anal. Mining **11**(1), 1–8 (2021). https://doi.org/10.1007/s13278-021-00766-8
5. Zafarani, R., Zhou, X., Shu, K., Liu, H.: Fake news research: theories, detection strategies, and open problems. In: Proceedings of the 25th ACM SIGKDD International Conference on Knowledge Discovery and Data Mining, pp. 3207–3208 (2019)
6. Zhou, X., Jain, A., Phoha, V.V., Zafarani, R.: Fake news early detection: a theory driven model. Digit. Threats: Res. Pract. **1**(2), 1–25 (2020)

7. Zhou, X., Mulay, A., Ferrara, E., Zafarani, R.: Recovery: a multimodal repository for covid-19 news credibility research. In: Proceedings of the 29th ACM International Conference on Information and Knowledge Management, pp. 3205–3212 (2020)

8. Zhou, X., Wu, J., Zafarani, R.: Safe: Similarity-aware multi-modal fake news detection. arXiv e-prints pp. arXiv–2003 (2020)

9. Zhou, X., Zafarani, R.: A survey of fake news: Fundamental theories, detection methods, and opportunities. ACM Comput. Surv. (CSUR) **53**(5), 1–40 (2020)

Reza Zafarani is an Assistant Professor of electrical engineering and computer science at Syracuse University. His research interests are in Data Mining, Machine Learning, Social Media Mining, and Social Network Analysis. His research has been published at major academic venues and highlighted in various scientific and news outlets. He is the principal author of *"Social Media Mining: An Introduction"* a textbook by Cambridge University Press and the associate editor for SIGKDD Explorations and Frontiers in communication. He is the winner of the NSF CAREER award, President's Award for Innovation, and outstanding teaching award at Arizona State University.

Contents

The Explanatory Gap in Algorithmic News Curation

Hendrik Heuer[(⊠)]

Institute for Information Management (ifib) & Centre for Media, Communication
and Information Research (ZeMKI), University of Bremen, Bremen, Germany
hheuer@uni-bremen.de

Abstract. Considering the large amount of available content, social
media platforms increasingly employ machine learning (ML) systems to
curate news. This paper examines how well different explanations help
expert users understand why certain news stories are recommended to
them. The expert users were journalists, who are trained to judge the
relevance of news. Surprisingly, none of the explanations are perceived
as helpful. Our investigation provides a first indication of a gap between
what is available to explain ML-based curation systems and what users
need to understand such systems. We call this the Explanatory Gap in
Machine Learning-based Curation Systems.

Keywords: Algorithmic transparency · Algorithmic experience ·
Recommender system · Algorithmic news curation · Machine learning

1 Introduction

Machine learning (ML)-based curation systems are frequently applied to suggest products, restaurants, movies, songs, and other content. Such systems have become a ubiquitous part of users' daily experience of information systems [25]. On social media sites like Facebook and Twitter, ML-based curation systems solve the challenging tasks of selecting, organizing, and presenting news from a variety of sources [12]. While curation is necessary considering the large number of users of social media sites and the immense number of available news stories, ML-based curation systems pose important challenges regarding algorithmic transparency and algorithmic experience [3,8,24,36]. In the past, news curation was a task predominantly performed by skilled journalists, who assessed the newsworthiness of content [48]. Increasingly, this task is performed by complex and opaque algorithms that lack transparency. This is problematic since social media platforms, which rely on ML-based curation systems, are becoming an important source of news [6,14,18]. Two-thirds of 18–24 year-olds worldwide rely on social media for news [33]. Facebook's News Feed is the canonical example of an ML-based curation system that is used daily by a large number of users. A large majority of U.S. adults using Facebook's News Feed thinks they have little (57%) or no control (28%) over the news curation system [44]. More than

© Springer Nature Switzerland AG 2021
J. Bright et al. (Eds.): MISDOOM 2021, LNCS 12887, pp. 1–15, 2021.
https://doi.org/10.1007/978-3-030-87031-7_1

half of the respondents also said they do not understand why certain posts are included by the ML-based curation system. Only every seventh person (14%) thinks that they understand the curation on Facebook very well.

This paper explores how the simplicity, intuitiveness, and interactivity of explanations influences users' understanding of personalized recommender systems for news. Despite the active research on adaptation and personalization, little is known about how to best implement explanations for such systems and how such explanations are perceived by users [31]. While researchers try to take aspects like novelty, diversity, unexpectedness, and utility into account for the evaluation of recommendation systems [25], a research gap exists regarding the understanding of explanations for personalized recommender systems. With this paper, we address this research gap and conduct a user study where expert users use an ML-based curation system. The system provides three types of ML explanations that we selected based on the design criteria simplicity, intuitiveness, and interactivity [9, 42].

We conducted a user study with 25 professional journalists who trained personalized curation system by rating news stories in blocks. The ML-based curation system included the following explanations: (1) system predictions grouped by the confusion matrix (intuitiveness), (2) performance metrics like accuracy, precision, and recall commonly used to evaluate machine learning systems (simplicity), and (3) an interactive ranking of the most important keywords according to the curation system (interactivity). Users were able to interact with the (3) ranking of keywords by changing the importance of individual words which changed the feature importance in the model. Participants used all three explanations six times. After reviewing the recommendations and explanations with varying levels of system performance, participants rated how well the explanations supported their understanding of the curation system and how helpful they found the explanations. We also compare their understanding of the curation system to how well they think they understand Facebook's News Feed. Our analysis provides a first indication of an explanatory gap between what is available to explain curation systems and what users need to understand such systems. This gap exists for all three explanations, regardless of whether they are designed to be simple, intuitive, or interactive.

2   Background

Adaptive systems for news personalization have a long history [5, 16, 41]. Facebook, as one of the most widely used ML-based curation systems, cites three signals that are used to predict and rank the relevance of the content: what kind of content it is, who posted it, and how users interact with the content [13]. In our investigation, we focus on the basic specialization use case of selecting news, i.e. we do not take postings from other users into account. Our research connects to Hamilton et al., who highlight the importance of studying where, when, and how users are made aware of algorithms and how the perception translates into knowledge about the process at hand [21]. Amershi et al. argue that explicitly studying the users of learning systems is critical to advancing the field [4].

This connects to a large body of research on explanations that are derived in specific contexts, but whose helpfulness is not evaluated in experimental user studies [38,45]. Konstan and Riedl identified the most important open research problems and key challenges of recommender systems. They argue that the user experience of such systems needs more attention [28]. For Konstan and Riedl, the user experience is the delivery of the recommendations to the user and the interaction of the user with those recommendations. This view is supported by Jugovac and Jannach, who found that a large body of research is focused on the problem of rating prediction and item ranking while other aspects receive comparatively little attention [26]. This paper focuses on the classification of news, not the ranking of news or the prediction of ratings.

In the context of ML-based curation systems, transparency is especially important since research showed that it positively influences users' trust in systems [25]. Eiband et al. analyzed 35,000+ app store reviews of three popular Android apps regarding interaction problems that can be attributed to algorithmic decision-making [11]. They investigate user reviews of the mobile applications of Facebook and Netflix, which both rely on ML-based curation systems. Their analysis shows how timely the call for more transparency and better explanations of curation systems is. Eiband et al. highlight the importance of user control and explanations of output. They identified problems with the curation algorithm, e.g. the biases enacted by the algorithm and the way the algorithm ranked the results. They also found that users want more control over their feed. Overall, the investigation highlights the importance of intuitive, simple, and interactive explanations, which motivated this research.

Despite a large consensus that explanations are helpful and that algorithmic transparency is important [8,15,47], the amount of empirical research that investigates explanations of curation systems in experimental user studies is limited, with a few notable exceptions focused on Facebook [36,37] and YouTube [2,23]. Furthermore, McNee et al. found that user satisfaction does not always correlate with high recommender accuracy [30]. They show that the evaluation of such systems can be classified as the similarity of recommendation lists, recommendation serendipity, and the importance of user needs and expectations in a recommendation [30]. Experimental studies in specific contexts are crucial because the context of recommender systems is known to shape the evaluation criteria of users [25]. We, therefore, focus on news recommendations. Prior research showed that the task of providing explanations for an ML-based curation system is difficult. Green et al. found that insufficient research has considered how the interactions between people and models influence human decisions [19]. This is especially important for news, which directly influence how people perceive the world and which can potentially affect their political opinions. Rader et al. investigated how explanations can support algorithmic transparency in the context of Facebook's News Feed [36]. They explored different explanation styles ranging from black-box scenarios describing the motivation of a system over white box scenarios that describing inputs and outputs of a system or how the system works. They found that all explanations made participants more aware of how the system works and helped them detect biases. At the same time, the explanations were not helping participants evaluate the correctness of the system's output, which directly informed our research questions about whether explanations improve expert users' understanding of the quality of ML-based curation systems. Their research motivated us to focus on explanations of the model as a whole and to design novel explanations that go beyond the different explanation styles they explored.

3   Method

We designed three explanations based on the design criteria simplicity, intuitiveness, and interactivity regarding their helpfulness in the context of ML-based curation systems. These explanations make it transparent to users how well the system they are interacting with performs and how well the recommendations of a system are personalized to the user. This study addresses the following research questions:

- Do explanations focused on simplicity, intuitiveness, and interactivity improve expert users' understanding of an ML-based curation system (RQ1)?
- Which of the explanations is perceived as the most helpful in understanding news recommendations (RQ2)?
- How does the ability to change the curation system affect system performance (RQ3)?

To answer these research questions, we conducted an online study with professional journalists who trained personalized ML-based curation systems. The study consisted of two parts: rating news articles and evaluating curation systems. Before the study, participants were asked basic demographic questions regarding gender, age, and highest education. In the study, participants rated individual news articles using a Tinder-like swiping interface. The swiping interface was explained with a video. Participants rated six blocks of 12 news stories. After each block, a new machine learning model was trained. We trained the models with different amounts of training data, ranging from 10 to 60 news stories for each of the 25 users. The ML systems were trained with an 80%-train-20%-test-split so that the amount of test data to compute accuracy, precision, and recall was proportional to the amount of training data. For the sixth system, 60 news stories were used to train the system and 12 news stories were used to evaluate it. To compute reliable ML statistics, we performed 5-fold cross-validation [32].

Participants were presented with personalized predictions by the systems and three explanations based on design considerations explained in the following section. At the end of the experiment – after having used the explanations six times – participants rated the helpfulness of the three explanations on an 11-point Likert scale. Participants also rated how well they understood why certain posts are included by the system and others are not. The possible answers included *"Not well at all"*, *"Not very well"*, *"Somewhat well"*, *"Very well"*, and

"Don't know". We compared this to how well the participants understood why certain posts are included in Facebook's News Feed, a widely used ML-based curation system that does not provide such explanations.

3.1 Sampling and Participants

Our sampling strategy was aimed at recruiting professional journalists who are an ideal target audience to compare different explanations of curation systems because journalists are familiar with the task of news curation. This connects to prior research with extreme users which showed that they can provide rich insights into issues like customization in communication apps and can be generalized to other users [7,10,20]. Journalists are trained to judge what content is relevant and whether the content provided is balanced and fair. To recruit journalists, we identified newsletters of associations of journalism and communication science as well as online groups focused on journalism on a career-oriented social network. We also contacted local news outlets through their executive editors and their press spokespeople. On all channels, we published the same call for participation. Each participant had a chance to win one of ten 10€ vouchers or to have 10€ donated to charity. Seventy-seven percent of participants decided to donate their incentive to charity. Through this self-selection sampling, we recruited 25 professional journalists from Germany. The mean age of participants was 41.76 years with a standard deviation of 12.76. The youngest participant was 26, the oldest participant was 70. Thirteen participants identified as male (52%), ten as female (40%). Two chose not to disclose their gender. Our sample is highly educated. The large majority of participants (84%) have a university degree. All participants had a high-school equivalent education. Regulatory requirements regarding the welfare, rights, and privacy of human subjects were followed.

3.2 Explanations for ML-Based Curation System

In the study, each participant trained a personalized news curation system on a binary text classification task. The system was trained using the ratings that the user provided. Users interacted with the ML-based curation system through a web application. The task of the curation system was to predict whether a news story is interesting to a particular user or not. We developed the curation system from scratch to be able to change the ML model. The system predicts the interest in a story (y) given the nouns $(x_{i:n})$ in the story. We selected the Gaussian Naïve Bayes classifier as one of the most efficient and effective inductive learning algorithms for classification [34,50]. The Gaussian Naïve Bayes classifier is a supervised ML algorithm that applies Bayes' theorem while assuming conditional independence between words [29]. The Gaussian Naïve Bayes classifier is based on conditional probability, which makes the classifiers efficient to compute, straightforward to directly manipulate, and comparatively easy to explain. To train the curation system, participants were presented with a diverse mix of randomly selected news articles, political articles, cultural articles as well

System Predictions

Correctly predicted as interesting (3)
1. Naturwald in Deutschland: Regierung verfehlt wohl Vorgabe Bis 2020 sollen fünf Prozent der Waldfläche in Deutschland für (...)
2. Der Tag kompakt: Das soziale Abschiebungspaket Das Geordnete-Rückkehr-Gesetz ist beschlossen ++ Linda Teuteberg soll FDP (...)
3. Nach Anschlägen in Sri Lanka: Wie sich Touristen verhalten sollten Nach derzeitigem Stand sind deutsche Urlauber unverse (...)

Correctly predicted as uninteresting (4)
1. Revierderby BVB vs. Schalke – Wie geht's aus? Am Samstag steht der große Revierschlager zwischen Borussia Dortmund und de (...)
2. Letzter Tatort mit Postel und Mommsen: Zum Abschied eine Heroinspritze voll ...

Performance Metrics

In total, you have rated 36 messages. Of these, 28 messages were randomly selected to train the system. The remaining 8 messages were used to calculate the information displayed here.

The system you trained assigned **87.50%** of the messages correctly.
Precision score: 100.00%. The percentage indicates how many of the messages predicted as relevant were relevant.
Recall score: 75.00%. The percentage indicates how many of the relevant messages were predicted by the system.

Influential Keywords

	schwach	mäßig	stark
01. jahrbuch			stark
02. usa			stark
03. wochenend			stark
04. mitgliedschaft			stark
05. anschlagshintergründen			stark
06. regierungschef			stark
07. tottenham			stark
08. euro			stark
09. kirchenbrand			stark
10. sheffield		mäßig	
11. werder		mäßig	
12. schwundstufe		mäßig	
13. altersempfehlungen		mäßig	
14. malen		mäßig	
15. regeln		mäßig	

Fig. 1. Three explanations were shown to journalists. 1. System Predictions, i.e. predictions grouped by the confusion matrix, 2. Performance Metrics like accuracy, precision, and recall. 3. Influential Keywords and whether their influence on the model is weak, moderate, or strong.

as articles about football. For this, we collected 413 recent news articles from the German public-service broadcaster (ARD) and the news magazine with the widest-circulation (DER SPIEGEL). Participants rated a subset of these articles. These ratings were then used to train the personalized curation systems. For both the rating and the training of the curation system, we used the nouns in the teaser of the article, which empirically provided sufficient information for the prediction task in our investigation.

In this study, we compare three explanations shown in Fig. 1 that we designed based on the design criteria simplicity (**System Predictions**), intuitiveness (**Performance Metrics**), and interactivity (**Influential Keywords**). The **System Predictions** explanation presents participants with all predictions made by a personalized ML-based curation system. Participants were shown the headlines of all news from the test set in the four groups of the confusion matrix [32]. These groups include true positives (t_p), true negatives (t_n), false positives (f_p), and false negatives (f_n). True positives (t_p) are interesting news stories that are correctly predicted as interesting news stories, true negatives (t_n) are uninteresting news stories correctly predicted as uninteresting. False positives (f_p) are uninteresting news stories that are predicted as interesting. False negatives (f_n) are interesting news falsely predicted as uninteresting. We included the system predictions as intuitive explanations because they present the predictions in a format that is similar to how news recommendations are encountered by users [4,32,35]. We also presented the participants with the three most important **Performance Metrics** for ML systems: accuracy, precision, and recall [17,22]. Accuracy is defined as the percentage of correctly predicted news, i.e. $\frac{t_p+t_n}{t_p+t_n+f_p+f_n}$. Accuracy is one of the most widely used ML metrics in textbooks [17,32]. We also included precision as the proportion of the predicted news that is relevant [39]: $\frac{t_p}{t_p+f_p}$. Recall is the proportion of interesting news covered by the predictions [39]: $\frac{t_p}{t_p+f_n}$. The performance metrics were selected for their simplicity. Accuracy, precision, and recall all provide a single number that indicates the performance of a system, thus reducing the complexity of evaluating the quality of a system to a single, comparable number. Participants were also presented with the Top-15 most **Influential Keywords** of the Naïve Bayes classifier. The most influential keywords are the words with the highest prior probability for the class *interesting*. To render the prior probabilities of the Naïve Bayes classifier more human-interpretable, we scaled the probabilities to values between 0 and 100. We classified the influence of a keyword on the prediction into the three categories weak, medium, and strong. Weak are keywords with a score smaller than 25. Medium keywords have a score between 25 and 50. Strong keywords have a score between 51 and 100. The thresholds were determined empirically based on the experience gained from training a large number of models. The Influential Keywords explanation was motivated by work on interactive machine learning and the explainability of machine learning [27,40,46]. The approach is modeled after the feature importance that can be computed for decision trees [32]. We implemented it as a Naïve Bayes classifier, which allowed us to directly manipulate the posterior probability of individual keywords. Since prior research shows that interactivity influences the user experience of ML systems [4,46,49], we also investigated how users interact with a curation system and how this affects system performance. Half of the participants were able to change the influence of the Top-15 keywords. Those with even IDs were able to change the influence of the keywords, those with odd IDs were not able to change the influence.

4   Results

We presented expert users with the three explanations shown in Fig. 1 and studied whether the three explanations support them in understanding the news recommendations they receive. The large majority (60%) of participants stated that their understanding of why news stories were included by the system was *"not very well"* (44%) or *"not well at all"* (16%). Every third participant (36%) said their understanding was at least *"somewhat well"*. This is worse than how well they understood why certain posts are recommended by Facebook's News Feed algorithm. For the News Feed, the majority (56%) self-assessed their understanding as *"not very well"* (48%) or *"not well at all"* (8%). This means that the three explanations did not have a measurable effect on the self-reported understanding of users. We also found no difference between those who were able to interact with the systems and those who were not. In the following, we compare the answers of the journalists in our study to the U.S. citizens surveyed by Pew Research Institute [44]. The majority of U.S. citizens (53%) regarded their understanding of Facebook's News Feed as *"not very well"* (33%) or *"not well at all"* (20%). A larger fraction of U.S. adults thought that their understanding of News Feed is *"somewhat well"* (32%). 14% regarded their understanding of

Table 1. The three explanations did not help participants understand the personalized curation systems in Study I. Participants rated the helpfulness from 0 (very little) to 10 (very much).

Helpfulness	Static			Interactive		
	$\overline{X}$	σ	Mdn	$\overline{X}$	σ	Mdn
System predictions	**4.67**	2.77	4.5	3.54	1.90	3.0
Performance metrics	2.67	1.67	2.0	3.62	2.18	4.0
Keywords	3.50	2.91	3.0	**3.85**	2.30	4.0

Table 2. The table shows that participants changing the influence of keywords (interactive) led to worse system performance.

System	Accuracy		Precision		Recall	
	$\overline{X}$	σ	$\overline{X}$	σ	$\overline{X}$	σ
Static	**78.71**	7.89	**75.53**	18.43	**77.17**	26.66
Interactive	65.87	18.02	53.09	30.66	62.00	39.49

the News Feed as *"very well"*. This implies that the explanations in our investigation did not improve how well participants understood the system and did not improve algorithmic transparency (RQ1) (Table 1).

Next, we review how the helpfulness of the explanations is perceived by the participants. Those who interacted with the keywords rated performance metrics like accuracy, precision, and recall as the least helpful (with an average rating of 2.67). System predictions, i.e. seeing the correct predictions as well as false positives and false negatives, were rated as most helpful (4.67). The keywords received an average rating of 3.50. Those who did not interact with the system rated the system predictions as least helpful (3.54) and the keywords as the most helpful (3.85). The performance metrics were rated as 3.62. All of these ratings are below the neutral condition of 5, which indicates that the helpfulness of all three explanations is perceived as low. We found no significant statistical differences between the explanations as measured by the Mann–Whitney U tests, which means that the differences between the ratings could be due to chance. We also found that the ability to interact with the system had no measurable effect. This means that none of the explanations were considered helpful by our participants (RQ2).

Table 2 shows that curation systems where participants changed the importance of keywords performed considerably worse than those where they did not (RQ3). Personalized ML-based curation systems without participant keywords have 12.84% better accuracy, 15.17% higher recall, and 22.44% better precision. This comparison is based on 5-fold cross-validation. Our in-depth analysis showed that interactive systems for which participants changed a small number of keywords expressing interest performed much better than systems trained by participants that assigned a large number of keywords expressing a lack of interest. One possible explanation for this could be that the keywords selected by participants are not suited to guide ML systems in capturing participants' interests. This is especially surprising considering the framing of the interaction. Participants were not able to freely choose keywords. They only reranked the keywords proposed by the curation system. Nevertheless, the changes they made led to worse system performance. This suggests that the keywords selected by the participants have detrimental effects on the prediction performance of the systems.

5 Discussion

We studied explanations in the context of algorithmic news curation. This means that our findings are particularly relevant for those who want to apply ML to recommend news or other content like books, songs, or videos. We found no difference between simple, intuitive, and interactive explanations. None of the three explanations were perceived as helpful by the expert users. Only the intuitive explanation that showed system predictions was rated close to the neutral condition of 5 on the 11-point rating scale. This could imply that the best way to explain an ML-based curation system would be showing the system predictions. This, however, would have some important disadvantages. Unlike ML metrics like accuracy, precision, and recall (simplicity), or the most influential keywords (interactivity), it is hard to compare two systems based on their predictions (intuitiveness). Moreover, the goal of news curation and other ML systems is automation. Evaluating systems by reviewing individual predictions requires a significant time investment. This means that even though system predictions are the most highly rated, they are the least practical of the explanations that we considered. One possible explanation for their appeal is that in contrast to the performance metrics and the influential keywords, the system predictions are directly interpretable and easy to understand. Correct predictions, false positives, and false negatives are straightforward to understand. Overall, our results imply that common strategies of exposing ML systems focused on accuracy, precision, and recall (simplicity) or the most influential keywords (interactivity) could be an overextension for users. We, therefore, conclude that intuitiveness is the best paradigm of the three that we tested, even though it was not rated highly in absolute terms. Further research is needed to corroborate this, but considering our highly educated sample of expert users who are familiar with the curation task, it would be surprising if less experienced users benefit from the more complex explanations.

The key takeaway of the paper is that none of the three explanations were provided as helpful. When users were able to interact with the systems, the performance of the system was much worse. This could imply that the keywords that are important to participants are not the keywords that are important for the curation system. This poses important challenges regarding the direct manipulation of ML-based curation systems and might limit the possibilities for the interaction with curation systems. This is especially problematic because the Gaussian Naïve Bayes classifier used in this investigation is a straightforward application of conditional probability, which means that the poor performance is not merely a limitation of this specific classifier. Our findings extend to other statistical machine learning classifiers based on conditional probability because they show that the mathematically important words do not correspond to the words that the user considered to be most important.

Our findings imply that the three approaches to expose curation systems are misguided and need to be reconsidered. None of the three explanations are perceived as helpful by our expert users. The explanations did not improve participants' understanding of the curation system. More than half of the participants said their understanding of the system is "not very well" (33%) or "not well at all" (20%). This is comparable to how well they think they understand Facebook's News Feed and how well Facebook's News Feed is understood by the average U.S. citizen [44]. This implies that the explanations did not improve understanding.

Our results indicate a lack of coincidence between the information that can be extracted from a curation system and the information that is meaningful to users. Based on these findings, we introduce the **Explanatory Gap in Machine Learning-based Curation Systems** to describe the gap between what is available to explain curation systems and what users need to understand such systems. This has important implications for a large body of research on how to explain ML systems [27,38,46]. The Explanatory Gap in Machine Learning-based Curation Systems connects to research on the semantic gap in multimedia [43] and the social-technical gap, which Ackerman defined as *"the great divide between what we know we must support socially and what we can support technically"* [1]. While the socio-technical gap concerns the lack of technical mechanisms to support the social world, we identified a similar gap regarding the lack of technical mechanisms to support individuals that face complex algorithmic systems. Like the social-technical gap, the Explanatory Gap in Machine Learning-based Curation Systems is unlikely to go away. It is a conceptual framing that can encourage researchers to better understand what is available to explain curation systems and what is needed by users. We hope to encourage further research on how to approach and manage this gap. The finding extends on prior research, e.g., by Rader et al. (2018) [36], who showed that their explanations did not help users evaluate the correctness of a system's output. However, Rader et al. found that the explanations can make users more aware of how an ML-based system works and that these explanations helped users detect biases. These findings are corroborated by our findings. The findings imply that explanations need to be very simple and easy to understand. Considering the complexity of ML systems, how to achieve this remains an important open question.

This paper is limited by two factors in particular. The professional experience of expert users like journalists could have shaped their perception of how news curation should work and what explanations they consider as helpful. While this potentially limits the generalizability of our findings, if expert users who are familiar with the task of news curation do not benefit from explanations, it is unlikely that users without this background will be able to benefit from the explanations. Our findings are also limited by the high level of education of our participants. The large majority of participants had a university degree (84%). However, if even this highly educated subset of the population did not understand these explanations, less educated participants are unlikely to understand them better. Furthermore, we compared our participants' understanding of Facebook's News Feed to a nationally representative sample of U.S. citizens [44] and found that our findings are generalizable beyond the expert users.

6   Conclusion

In this paper, we introduce the Explanatory Gap in Machine Learning-based Curation Systems which describes the gap between what is available to explain ML-based curation systems and what users need to understand such systems. To improve users' understanding of curation systems and to inform algorithmic transparency research, we need further research that explores how such systems should be exposed to users and how the predictions of the systems can be explained. We hope to motivate further experimental studies that explore explanations with real-world tasks like news curation. Future work could investigate how the helpfulness of such explanations is perceived when they are used over a long period, e.g., days, months, or years. The findings indicate that explanations like the most important keywords and interactivity could be an overextension for users. Further research on how well users can understand machine learning systems and, by extension, statistics, would be beneficial. We propose conducting within-subject studies to advance ML explanations and algorithmic transparency. In addition to that, qualitative investigations are needed to explore why the explanations are not perceived as helpful by users. Explorative design studies will be crucial to examine what kind of explanations can help users understand ML-based curation systems.

References

1. Ackerman, M.S.: The intellectual challenge of CSCW: the gap between social requirements and technical feasibility. Hum.-Comput. Interact. **15**(2), 179–203 (2000). https://doi.org/10.1207/S15327051HCI1523_5
2. Alvarado, O., Heuer, H., Vanden Abeele, V., Breiter, A., Verbert, K.: Middle-aged video consumers' beliefs about algorithmic recommendations on YouTube. Proc. ACM Hum.-Comput. Interact. **4**(CSCW2) (2020). https://doi.org/10.1145/3415192
3. Alvarado, O., Waern, A.: Towards algorithmic experience: initial efforts for social media contexts. In: Proceedings of the 2018 CHI Conference on Human Factors in Computing Systems. CHI 2018, pp. 286:1–286:12. ACM, New York (2018). https://doi.org/10.1145/3173574.3173860, http://doi.acm.org/10.1145/3173574.3173860
4. Amershi, S., Cakmak, M., Knox, W.B., Kulesza, T.: Power to the people: the role of humans in interactive machine learning. AI Mag. **35**(4), 105–120 (2014)

5. Ardissono, L., Console, L., Torre, I.: An adaptive system for the personalized access to news. AI Commun. **14**(3), 129–147 (2001)
6. Bakshy, E., Rosenn, I., Marlow, C., Adamic, L.A.: The role of social networks in information diffusion. CoRR abs/1201.4145 (2012). http://arxiv.org/abs/1201.4145
7. Choe, E.K., Lee, N.B., Lee, B., Pratt, W., Kientz, J.A.: Understanding quantified-selfers' practices in collecting and exploring personal data. In: Proceedings of the SIGCHI Conference on Human Factors in Computing Systems. CHI 2014, pp. 1143–1152. ACM, New York (2014). https://doi.org/10.1145/2556288.2557372, http://doi.acm.org/10.1145/2556288.2557372
8. Diakopoulos, N., Koliska, M.: Algorithmic transparency in the news media. Digit. J. **5**(7), 809–828 (2017). https://doi.org/10.1080/21670811.2016.1208053
9. Dix, A., Finlay, J., Abowd, G.D., Beale, R.: Human Computer Interaction, 3rd edn. Pearson Prentice Hall, Harlow (2003)
10. Djajadiningrat, J.P., Gaver, W.W., Fres, J.W.: Interaction relabelling and extreme characters: methods for exploring aesthetic interactions. In: Proceedings of the 3rd Conference on Designing Interactive Systems: Processes, Practices, Methods, and Techniques. DIS 2000, pp. 66–71. ACM, New York (2000). https://doi.org/10.1145/347642.347664, http://doi.acm.org/10.1145/347642.347664
11. Eiband, M., Völkel, S.T., Buschek, D., Cook, S., Hussmann, H.: When people and algorithms meet: user-reported problems in intelligent everyday applications. In: Proceedings of the 24th International Conference on Intelligent User Interfaces. IUI 2019, pp. 96–106. ACM, New York (2019). https://doi.org/10.1145/3301275.3302262, http://doi.acm.org/10.1145/3301275.3302262
12. Eslami, M., et al.: "I always assumed that I wasn't really that close to [her]": reasoning about invisible algorithms in news feeds. In: Proceedings of the 33rd Annual ACM Conference on Human Factors in Computing Systems. CHI 2015, pp. 153–162. ACM, New York (2015). https://doi.org/10.1145/2702123.2702556, http://doi.acm.org/10.1145/2702123.2702556
13. Facebook: Facebook News Feed (2018). https://newsfeed.fb.com/
14. Knight Foundation: American views: Trust, media and democracy, January 2018. https://knightfoundation.org/reports/american-views-trust-media-and-democracy
15. Geiger, R.S.: Beyond opening up the black box: investigating the role of algorithmic systems in Wikipedian organizational culture. Big Data Soc. **4**(2) (2017). https://doi.org/10.1177/2053951717730735, http://journals.sagepub.com/doi/10.1177/2053951717730735
16. Gena, C., Grillo, P., Lieto, A., Mattutino, C., Vernero, F.: When personalization is not an option: an in-the-wild study on persuasive news recommendation. Information **10**(10) (2019). https://doi.org/10.3390/info10100300, https://www.mdpi.com/2078-2489/10/10/300
17. Goodfellow, I., Bengio, Y., Courville, A.: Deep Learning. The MIT Press, Cambridge (2016)
18. Gottfried, J., Shearer, E.: News Use Across Social Media Platforms 2016, May 2016. http://www.journalism.org/2016/05/26/news-use-across-social-media-platforms-2016/
19. Green, B., Chen, Y.: The principles and limits of algorithm-in-the-loop decision making. Proc. ACM Hum.-Comput. Interact. **3**(CSCW), 50:1–50:24 (2019). https://doi.org/10.1145/3359152, http://doi.acm.org/10.1145/3359152
20. Griggio, C.F., McGrenere, J., Mackay, W.: Customizations and expression breakdowns in ecosystems of communication apps. In: CSCW 2019, Austin, Texas (2019)

21. Hamilton, K., Karahalios, K., Sandvig, C., Eslami, M.: A path to understanding the effects of algorithm awareness. In: CHI 2014 Extended Abstracts on Human Factors in Computing Systems. CHI EA 2014, pp. 631–642. ACM, New York (2014). https://doi.org/10.1145/2559206.2578883, http://doi.acm.org/10.1145/2559206.2578883

22. Heuer, H., Breiter, A.: More than accuracy: towards trustworthy machine learning interfaces for object recognition. In: Proceedings of the 28th ACM Conference on User Modeling, Adaptation and Personalization. UMAP 2020, pp. 298–302. Association for Computing Machinery, New York (2020). https://doi.org/10.1145/3340631.3394873

23. Heuer, H., Hoch, H., Breiter, A., Theocharis, Y.: Auditing the biases enacted by YouTube for political topics in Germany. In: Proceedings of Mensch Und Computer 2021. MuC 2021. Association for Computing Machinery, New York (2021). https://doi.org/10.1145/3473856.3473864

24. Heuer, H., Jarke, J., Breiter, A.: Machine learning in tutorials - universal applicability, underinformed application, and other misconceptions. Big Data Soc. 8(1), 20539517211017590 (2021). https://doi.org/10.1177/20539517211017593

25. Jannach, D., Resnick, P., Tuzhilin, A., Zanker, M.: Recommender systems - beyond matrix completion. Commun. ACM 59(11), 94–102 (2016). https://doi.org/10.1145/2891406. http://doi.acm.org/10.1145/2891406

26. Jugovac, M., Jannach, D.: Interacting with recommenders - overview and research directions. ACM Trans. Interact. Intell. Syst. 7(3), 10:1–10:46 (2017). https://doi.org/10.1145/3001837, http://doi.acm.org/10.1145/3001837

27. Kim, B.: Interactive and interpretable machine learning models for human machine collaboration. Ph.D. thesis, Massachusetts Institute of Technology (2015)

28. Konstan, J.A., Riedl, J.: Recommender systems: from algorithms to user experience. User Model. User-Adap. Inter. 22(1), 101–123 (2012). https://doi.org/10.1007/s11257-011-9112-x

29. Maron, M.E.: Automatic indexing: an experimental inquiry. J. ACM 8(3), 404–417 (1961). https://doi.org/10.1145/321075.321084. http://doi.acm.org/10.1145/321075.321084

30. McNee, S.M., Riedl, J., Konstan, J.A.: Being accurate is not enough: how accuracy metrics have hurt recommender systems. In: CHI 2006 Extended Abstracts on Human Factors in Computing Systems. CHI EA 2006, pp. 1097–1101. ACM, New York (2006). https://doi.org/10.1145/1125451.1125659, http://doi.acm.org/10.1145/1125451.1125659

31. Millecamp, M., Htun, N.N., Conati, C., Verbert, K.: To explain or not to explain: the effects of personal characteristics when explaining music recommendations. In: Proceedings of the 24th International Conference on Intelligent User Interfaces. IUI 2019, pp. 397–407. ACM, New York (2019). https://doi.org/10.1145/3301275.3302313, http://doi.acm.org/10.1145/3301275.3302313

32. Müller, A., Guido, S.: Introduction to Machine Learning with Python: A Guide for Data Scientists. O'Reilly Media (2016). https://books.google.de/books?id=vbQlDQAAQBAJ

33. Newman, N., Fletcher, R., Kalogeropoulos, A., Levy, D.A., Nielsen, R.K.: Reuters Institute Digital News Report 2019 (2019). http://www.digitalnewsreport.org/survey/2019/overview-key-findings-2019/

34. Ng, A.Y., Jordan, M.I.: On discriminative vs. generative classifiers: a comparison of logistic regression and Naive Bayes. In: Dietterich, T.G., Becker, S., Ghahramani, Z. (eds.) Advances in Neural Information Processing Systems 14, pp. 841–848. MIT Press (2002). http://papers.nips.cc/paper/2020-on-discriminative-vs-generative-classifiers-a-comparison-of-logistic-regression-and-naive-bayes.pdf

35. Powers, D.M.W.: Evaluation: from precision, recall and F-measure to ROC, informedness, markedness & correlation. J. Mach. Learn. Technol. **2**(1), 37–63 (2011)

36. Rader, E., Cotter, K., Cho, J.: Explanations as mechanisms for supporting algorithmic transparency. In: Proceedings of the 2018 CHI Conference on Human Factors in Computing Systems. CHI 2018, pp. 103:1–103:13. ACM, New York (2018). https://doi.org/10.1145/3173574.3173677, http://doi.acm.org/10.1145/3173574.3173677

37. Rader, E., Gray, R.: Understanding user beliefs about algorithmic curation in the Facebook news feed. In: Proceedings of the 33rd Annual ACM Conference on Human Factors in Computing Systems. CHI 2015, pp. 173–182. ACM, New York (2015). https://doi.org/10.1145/2702123.2702174, http://doi.acm.org/10.1145/2702123.2702174

38. Ribeiro, M.T., Singh, S., Guestrin, C.: "Why should i trust you?": explaining the predictions of any classifier. In: Proceedings of the 22nd ACM SIGKDD International Conference on Knowledge Discovery and Data Mining. KDD 2016, pp. 1135–1144. ACM, New York (2016). https://doi.org/10.1145/2939672.2939778, http://doi.acm.org/10.1145/2939672.2939778

39. Rijsbergen, C.J.V.: Information Retrieval, 2nd edn. Butterworth-Heinemann, Newton (1979)

40. Selvaraju, R.R., Das, A., Vedantam, R., Cogswell, M., Parikh, D., Batra, D.: Grad-CAM: why did you say that? Visual explanations from deep networks via gradient-based localization. CoRR abs/1610.02391 (2016). http://arxiv.org/abs/1610.02391

41. Sheidin, J., Lanir, J., Kuflik, T., Bak, P.: Visualizing spatial-temporal evaluation of news stories. In: Proceedings of the 22nd International Conference on Intelligent User Interfaces Companion. IUI 2017 Companion, pp. 65–68. ACM, New York (2017). https://doi.org/10.1145/3030024.3040984, http://doi.acm.org/10.1145/3030024.3040984

42. Shneiderman, B., Plaisant, C.: Designing the User Interface: Strategies for Effective Human-Computer Interaction, 4th edn. Pearson Addison Wesley, Reading (2004)

43. Smeulders, A.W.M., Worring, M., Santini, S., Gupta, A., Jain, R.: Content-based image retrieval at the end of the early years. IEEE Trans. Pattern Anal. Mach. Intell. **22**(12), 1349–1380 (2000). https://doi.org/10.1109/34.895972

44. Smith, A.: Many Facebook users don't understand its news feed (2019). http://www.pewresearch.org/fact-tank/2018/09/05/many-facebook-users-dont-understand-how-the-sites-news-feed-works/

45. Strobelt, H., Gehrmann, S., Huber, B., Pfister, H., Rush, A.M.: Visual analysis of hidden state dynamics in recurrent neural networks. CoRR abs/1606.07461 (2016). http://arxiv.org/abs/1606.07461

46. Stumpf, S., et al.: Interacting meaningfully with machine learning systems: three experiments. Int. J. Hum.-Comput. Stud. **67**(8), 639–662 (2009). https://doi.org/10.1016/j.ijhcs.2009.03.004. http://www.sciencedirect.com/science/article/pii/S1071581909000457

47. Tintarev, N., Masthoff, J.: Evaluating the effectiveness of explanations for recommender systems: methodological issues and empirical studies on the impact of personalization. User Model. User-Adap. Inter. **22**(4–5), 399–439 (2012). https://doi.org/10.1007/s11257-011-9117-5. https://link.springer.com/article/10.1007/s11257-011-9117-5

48. Trielli, D., Diakopoulos, N.: Search as news curator: the role of Google in shaping attention to news information. In: Proceedings of the 2019 CHI Conference on Human Factors in Computing Systems. CHI 2019, pp. 453:1–453:15. ACM, New York (2019). https://doi.org/10.1145/3290605.3300683, http://doi.acm.org/10.1145/3290605.3300683

49. Tullio, J., Dey, A.K., Chalecki, J., Fogarty, J.: How it works: a field study of non-technical users interacting with an intelligent system. In: Proceedings of the SIGCHI Conference on Human Factors in Computing Systems, pp. 31–40. ACM (2007)

50. Zhang, H.: The optimality of Naive Bayes. In: Barr, V., Markov, Z. (eds.) Proceedings of the Seventeenth International Florida Artificial Intelligence Research Society Conference (FLAIRS 2004). AAAI Press (2004)

Examining Linguistic Biases in Telegram with a Game Theoretic Analysis

Sviatlana Höhn[1]([⊠])[iD], Nicholas Asher[2][iD], and Sjouke Mauw[1][iD]

[1] DCS/SnT, University of Luxembourg, Esch-sur-Alzette, Luxembourg
{sviatlana.hoehn,sjouke.mauw}@uni.lu
[2] IRIT, Toulouse, France
Nicholas.Asher@irit.fr

Abstract. Selective formulations and selective reporting of facts in political news are deliberately used to create particular identities of different political sides. This becomes evident in media dialogue reporting about political conflicts. In contrast to most NLP-based studies of linguistic bias, we engage critically with its nature, aiming at a later de-biasing or at least raising awareness about linguistic bias in political news. We found inspiration in conversation analysis (CA), membership categorisation analysis (MCA) and a game-theoretic approach to discourse called epistemic message exchange (ME) games. We identified three types of bias: selective reports about facts, selective formulations when reporting about the same facts, and different histories built up by the differences in the first two. We extend the epistemic ME games model with findings from a qualitative study.

Keywords: Linguistic bias · Epistemic message exchange games · Political news · Membership categorization analysis

1 Introduction

Different political parties use different formulations to describe the same events in order to create different opinions and attract voters. Neutral, unbiased descriptions are difficult to find. The most recent critical survey on bias in NLP by Blodgett et al. [7] emphasises that the majority of scholarly articles on NLP-based bias analysis or detection fail to engage critically with the nature of bias, which is a multidisciplinary issue.

Prior academic research describes three types of bias in media: (1) the *selection* bias (gatekeeping) by which a channel selects whether an issue needs reporting or not; (2) the *coverage* bias in which a channel chooses how much space an issue is allocated; and (3) the *framing* bias, also called *linguistic* bias in which a channel chooses a particular way to describe a fact or an event. While multiple academic works report about statistical approaches to bias detection relying on word similarities (e.g. works cited in [7]), they

We thank the ANR PRCI grant SLANT, the Luxembourgish National Research Fund, INTER-SLANT 13320890 and the 3IA Institute ANITI funded by the ANR-19-PI3A-0004 grant for research support.

J. Bright et al. (Eds.): MISDOOM 2021, LNCS 12887, pp. 16–32, 2021.
https://doi.org/10.1007/978-3-030-87031-7_2

rarely take the sequentiality of media discourse into account. The role of the discourse or conversational structure in the linguistic bias still needs analysis.

Our **research objective** is to evaluate and to extend a formal model of linguistic bias [3] that takes into account the dynamics and structure of discourse to descriptions of events. For our empirical study, we have focused on descriptions of events in Belorussian Telegram channels—including official Belorussian news channels ONT NEWS, BelTA and Pool Pervogo, and opposition channels BelSAT, Belarus Seychas, and TUT.BY with posts in Russian and Belorussian languages. The analysis is mostly based on the dataset of 140.388 Telegram posts (76.918 opposition and 63.470 state); 109.721 posts contain text (58.976 opposition and 50.745 state). We created this dataset using the "Export chat history" function of the Telegram desktop application[1]. The data cover messages from 1.08.2020 (shortly before presidential elections in Belarus) to 14.04.2021 (date of the download). While "established" social media (e.g. Facebook, YouTube) played a huge role in political protests a decade ago, current political movements find main support in messengers like Telegram [1] and new social networks like TikTok [9]. Researchers need to catch up with these changes.

We use a mixed-method approach to data analysis as explained in Sect. 2 to identify types of biases in our dataset, and to validate the game-theoretic model [5]. Following [7], we explicitly include the effect of linguistic bias in our formal model, i.e. what bias is harmful in what way and to whom. We show that the formal model explains causal factors of linguistic bias in our data. We also show how the model captures aspects of approaches to bias in membership categorisation analysis, in particular the important function of labeling.

Linguistic labels help to give content to *types*, a key element, in epistemic ME games. Labelling is also a strategic device. In political news, biases are used purposefully and consciously; labelling is not systematic, but invented and opportunistic [18]. We also show how labels evolve over time by considering the extended discourse structure of the interactions between different media sources.

After the intuitive explanation of the epistemic ME games in Sect. 2, we present the formalisation in Sect. 3. We evaluate the formal model in Sect. 4. We show in Sect. 4.1 how category choices manipulate meaning in order to construct particular identities for various actors and make actions towards particular social categories accountable [12]. Section 4.2 shows on examples from our dataset that it is nearly impossible to find a neutral, unbiased description of events in media associated with one or another side of a political conflict. Section 4.3 shows how two identified prototypical types called PROTESTER and POLICE interact. Section 4.4 shows how unbiased labels become biased over time and how bias becomes more and more stable over time. We discuss the results in Sect. 5.

2   The Basic Model and Method

Most NLP-based bias detection models work with the definition of linguistic bias as *"a systematic asymmetry in word choice" reflecting "social-category cognitions"* [6]. The

---

[1] Available at https://github.com/sviatlanahoehn/BelElect.

key idea is that, using social category labels for individuals communicates category and stereotype-congruent information, which can be benevolent or harmful [10].

For us, linguistic bias manifests itself not only at the lexical level but at the discursive level as well. In addition, linguistic bias is the product not only of choices of the author of a text but also of its interpreter, and the choices the author makes are geared to how the interpreters will understand them. This reflects a theme of conversational analysis, on which speakers construct their utterances for a specific recipient in a specific context (*recipient design* as set of recipient-directed practices and *membership categorisation* as analysis of assigned categories) [11, Ch.2]. To frame the issue of bias, let us suppose that our author $\mathcal{A}$ wants to convey information about some event or object e, which we formalize as the set of formulas $F(x)$, satisfiable by e. We say *satisfiable* because $\mathcal{A}$ may of course choose to convey falsehoods about e; our only constraint is that $\mathcal{A}$ only conveys content that is logically and semantically consistent (i.e. does not violate selectional or other restrictions).

As shown in [3], an author's bias reveals itself in part in what set of facts $C_F(x) \subset F(x)$ about e she chooses to convey, what lexical choices she makes to describe $C_F(x)$ (lexical semantics), how those lexical contents combine together (compositional semantics) and how they weave their descriptions of elements of $C_F(x)$ into a consistent and coherent story, narrative or what [5] call a *history*. To build a history, the author must link the chosen basic facts together with semantic or what are known as *discourse relations* that convey causal, temporal, or thematic information. A narrative should make clear how each object or event in $C_F(x)$ chosen by the author fits into a coherent whole. The author's bias thus manifests itself at the level of lexical semantics, compositional semantics and discourse semantics.

Screenshot Example 1   Screenshot Example 2

Example 1. ONT 15.11.2020 12:48 https://t.me/ontnews/21504

On Sunday, ordinary people want to rest, but the protesters don't think about them, the people who live in these houses! Noise, yelling, wild chants and car horns, a virtually completely barricaded yard and entrances to it... A typical example of how an aggressive minority can poison the life of an entire city.

To give an illustration, compare Example 1 posted by a Belorussian state news channel ONT and Example 2 posted by an opposition news channel TUT.BY. The screenshots from the videos that were part of the messages look very similar, they were recorded at the same time and at the same place, the so-called Square of Changes[2]. The corresponding text messages, however, emphasize different aspects of the events reported (framing bias). While Example 1 complains about noise caused by "an aggressive minority" on a weekend, Example 2 reports about people who chanted the opposition slogans and refers to the video, leaving the interpretation to the reader; it does not mention "virtually completely barricaded yard and entrances to it". Example 3 posted by the same opposition news channel reports about law enforcement bodies who use stun grenades. The state channel ONT does not say anything about using stun grenades on that day.

Example 2. TUT.BY 15.11.2020 12:04 https://t.me/tutby_official/19429
Minsk. This is what the Square of Changes looked like at 1:45 p.m.
People chanted "We believe, we can, we win!"

Example 3. TUT.BY 15.11.2020 12:21 https://t.me/tutby_official/19429
Law enforcement bodies arrived at the "Square of Changes" in Minsk. They use stun grenades - eyewitnesses report four explosions.

An additional parameter in bias comes from the interpreter. The author may choose ambiguous expressions or leave certain discourse connections unspecified. It is then the interpreter's role to resolve the ambiguities and create a coherent history about *e*. It is in the interaction of author and interpreter choices that the game theoretic side of bias becomes clear. For $\mathcal{A}$ will make her choices in the light of how she thinks her interpreter I will construe those choices, in particular how I chooses to resolve the ambiguities and to fill in the underspecified elements. This part of the model reflects the requirements of minimality (not to overspecify) and recognisability (provide enough information for the recipient's sense-making), as explained in, for instance, [11, Ch. 2]. In turn I will make her choices based on her beliefs about $\mathcal{A}$ and the context. Biases are concretized and conveyed via the interaction of $\mathcal{A}$'s and I's conversational strategies.

Our model of bias comes from the game-theoretic framework of Epistemic Message Exchange (ME) games [5], but it has links to membership categorisation analysis (MCA) [21, 23] and conversation analysis (CA) [22]. In particular we analyse labels and rights and obligations that those labels evoke [20, 21]. Labels incorporate a range of prototypical associations that authors and their interlocutors can exploit to draw inferences. Categories may have constitutive features that at least partially define the denotation of the label, but also occasioned features, features that members of the category on occasion possess that one can exploit for strategic purposes. We also analyse the sequential structure of media discourse. Although the contributions of our prototypical speakers PROTESTER and POLICE are not adjacent, they are analysably *next* to each other, i.e. they are type-fitted and the speakers of each *second* orient to their *firsts* [25].

CA, and MCA in particular, have been successfully applied to understand identity construction in language [13, 17]; but it is difficult to formalize let alone operationalize. Epistemic ME games, on the other hand, build on a sophisticated formal analysis of discourse and conversational structure, which permits us to capture important insights of CA and MCA for bias [5]. Following [12, p. 6], "a warranted analysis of the contextual

---

[2] https://en.wikipedia.org/wiki/Square_of_Changes.

meaning of the categorisation is based only on evidence in the text analysed." We have tried to interpret the use of labels cautiously.

3   The Formal Model of Bias

The intuitive picture presented in Sect. 2 is not yet an explanatory model. To do this we follow [5] and formalize the intuitive picture in the following way. A Message Exchange (ME) game involves two players 0 and 1, each with a set of discourse moves, V_0 and V_1. Formally,

Definition 1. *A* Message Exchange game (ME game), G, *is a tuple* $((V_0 \cup V_1)^\infty, \mathcal{J})$ *where $\mathcal{J}$ is a Jury.*

In the definition, the Jury determines which player (or players) has achieved her goal in the conversation; in other words, it fixes the winning conditions in an objective fashion for the players. The Jury is typically an agent distinct from the players 0 and 1 of a ME game, but we can also sometimes identify the Jury with one of the players.

Definition 2 (Jury). *The* Jury *of an ME game is a tuple* $\mathcal{J} = (Win_0, Win_1)$ *where* $Win_i \subset (V_0 \cup V_1)^\infty$ *for each i.*

The notion of a Jury also helps capture the intuition that the interpretation of what happened in a conversation may not solely be a matter of what the conversationalists themselves think; each conversationalist might remember or "spin" the conversation in such a way so as to show that she had won.

An ME game proceeds in turns where, by convention, player 0 starts the game by playing move x_1, player 1 follows with x_2, player 0 then plays x_3 and so on. These moves are understood to be formulas of a language V representing the semantic content of natural language conversational turns; as such they will include not only formulas representing individual items in $C_F(e)$ but also the semantic relations holding between them, as in Semantic Discourse Representation Theory (SDRT) [4,5]. This results in the sequence $x_1x_2x_3 \dots$. Given our language V, this sequence is a concatenation of formulas from $V_0 \cup V_1$, where concatenation is viewed as conjunction. Consider the conversation between two conversationalists, our 0 and 1 in Example 4.

Example 4. 30.09.2020 14:15 Belarus Seychas https://t.me/belarusseichas/12032
Basketball player Elena Levchenko was sentenced to 15 days of administrative arrest. Shouts of "Shame" were heard in the hall.

(1)   a. $\rho_1 = (\mathcal{B}asketball\ player\ \mathcal{E}lena\ Levchenko\ was\ sentenced\ to\ 15\ days\ of\ administrative\ arrest.\ \mathcal{S}houts\ of\ "\mathcal{S}hame"\ were\ heard\ in\ the\ hall,\ 0)$

       b. $\rho_2 = (\mathcal{D}o\ you\ know\ why\ they\ shouted\ "\mathcal{S}hame"?,\ 1)$

Assume player 0 plays the sequence ρ_1. This sequence yields a formula of V_0— a pair consisting of the V formula together with the index 0 for player $[(\langle \pi_1 : \phi_1 \rangle \wedge \langle \pi_2 : \phi_2 \rangle \wedge \mathcal{R}(\pi_1, \pi_2)), 0)]$ where π_1 and π_2 mark *elementary discourse units* or EDUs given by the two sentences in (1-a), and $\mathcal{R}$ is a relation on such discourses. Player 1 then plays the sequence ρ_2 which translates into a formula of V_1, itself a pair consisting of a formula in V for the EDU introduced by the question paired with 1. This results in the sequence $\rho_1\rho_2$. This motivates the following definition of a play of an ME game.

Definition 3 (Play). *A* play ρ *of an ME game is a sequence in* $(V_0 \cup V_1)$.

ρ can be underspecified like that for ρ_1 above where the semantic connection between the sentencing and the shouts is left open. This motivates the following:

Definition 4 (History). *A* history h *of an ME game is a play that is a semantically fully specified unit.*

Given a play ρ, $\mathcal{H}(\rho)$ denotes the set of all histories generated by specifying or removing ambiguities in ρ. $\mathcal{H}(\rho)$ can contain multiple, distinct, even incompatible histories. For example there are at least two possible histories for the play ρ_1 in (1-a): (i) one in which shouts of shame are a Result of the *sentencing* by the institution—and hence the shouts of shame are directed towards the sentencing institution; (ii) one in which the shouts of shame are an Acknowledgment and Comment on the player's behavior that led to the sentencing and thus directed towards her.

(2)   Histories for ρ_1 in (1)

    a. $h_1(\rho_1) = [(\langle \pi_a : \phi_a \rangle \wedge \langle \pi_b : \phi_b \rangle \wedge \mathsf{res}(\pi_a, \pi_b)), 0]$

    b. $h_2(\rho_1) = [(\langle \pi_a : \phi_a \rangle \wedge \langle \pi_b : \phi_b \rangle \wedge \mathsf{ack}(\pi_a, \pi_b)), 0]$

Let $|\rho|$ denote the number of turns in a play ρ and $|\mathcal{H}|$ denote the same for $\mathcal{H}$. We let $\mathcal{P}$ (resp. $\mathcal{H}$) denote the set of all plays (resp. histories).

Definition 5 (Winning plays/histories). *A play* ρ *(or history* h*) is said to be* winning *for player i if* $\rho \in Win_i$ *(or* h $\in Win_i$*).*

Players' strategies are an important element for developing and conveying biases. A strategy of player *i* tells us how *i* reacts to player $1-i$'s moves.

Definition 6 (Pure strategy). *A pure strategy* σ_i *for player i in an ME game is a function from the set of* $(1-i)$*-plays to moves in* V_i^+*, the finite positive sequences in* V_i^**. That is,* $\sigma_i : \mathcal{P}_{(1-i)} \to V_i^+$*. Let* S_i *denote the set of strategies for player i and let* $S = S_0 \times S_1$*.*

Let $\rho = x_0 x_1 \ldots$ be a play in an ME game and let $\rho_j = x_0 x_1 \ldots x_j$ for $j > 0$ be the set of prefixes of ρ. We say that ρ conforms to a strategy σ_i of player *i* if for every $(1-i)$-play ρ_j, $x_{j+1} = \sigma_i(\rho_j)$. Given a finite play ρ, we let S_i^ρ denote the set of all strategies σ_i of player *i* such that ρ conforms to σ_i and let S^ρ denote the set of all strategy pairs (σ_0, σ_1) such that ρ conforms to (σ_0, σ_1).

    To see some examples of strategies, let's return to (1). Suppose 0 has played ρ_1; one strategy of 1 is to play a clarification question $\rho_{2'}$ like *did you mean that the shouts of "Shame" were addressed to the court?* to understand better which history $h_1(\rho_1)$ of (2-a) or $h_2(\rho_1)$ of (2-b) was intended. Another strategy is to assume that the intended history was (2-a) and to ask for an explanation of why there were shouts of "Shame". It is this latter strategy that conforms to the actual play in ρ_1, ρ_2 of (1).

    We now turn to the epistemic component of ME games. Players' beliefs, or the subjective probabilities they assign to plays, moves, and strategies affect how they reason in an ME game, i.e. what they say or how they react to some conversational turn. And for this, a player's beliefs must include beliefs about other players's strategies and beliefs about them. This nested structure of higher order beliefs (beliefs about beliefs) can be expressed in different ways, but a natural way to do this is to exploit the type of a player [14]. The type T_i of a player i is a property of the player that encodes his behaviour, the way he strategizes, his personal biases, etc. The $i-types$ for a player i are the possible properties, possible behaviors relevant to the ME game, that i could instantiate. Rubrics like "protester" and "police" describe types that we will use below. We will assume probability distributions, written $\Delta(A)$, for sets A that could be sets of types or of strategies. We will assume types for the players of our game as well as of the Jury.

Crucial to our view of bias, the beliefs of the players affect what content they get from a message and how those messages affect their beliefs. Following [5], we separate out the effect of types both on beliefs about other players and on interpretations of a conversation that result in particular histories.

Definition 7 (Belief function). *For every play* $\rho \in \mathcal{P}$ *the* (first order) belief $\hat{\beta}_i^\rho$ *of player* i *at* ρ *is a pair of functions* $\hat{\beta}_i^\rho = (\beta_i^\rho, \xi_i^\rho)$ *where* β_i^ρ *is the* belief function *and* ξ_i^ρ *is the* interpretation function *defined as:*

$$\beta_i^\rho : T_i \times \mathcal{H}(\rho) \rightarrow \Delta(T_{(1-i)}) \times \Delta(S_{(1-i)}^\rho) \times \Delta(T_J)$$
$$\xi_i^\rho : T_i \times T_{(1-i)} \times T_J \rightarrow \Delta(\mathcal{H}(\rho))$$

The (first order) belief $\hat{\beta}_J^\rho$ *of the Jury is described by a similar pair of functions.*

Intuitively, by fixing a type for the players and the Jury, the respective interpretation function says how they interpret the current play; that is, what are the probabilities that they assign to each possible history arising from the current play. The belief function returns the beliefs about the types and the strategies of the other players and/or the Jury given a history and a particular player type; together the interpretation and belief functions show a *codependence between beliefs and interpretation.*[3]

We now have the pieces to define our tool for analyzing linguistic bias:

Definition 8. *An* Epistemic Message Exchange game (Epistemic ME game), $\mathcal{G}$, *is an ME game, with set of types for the players and the Jury and belief functions for* 0, 1 *and the Jury, as defined in Definition 7.*

In some cases, the beliefs or the interpretations of the players or the Jury may be independent of one or more components or those components may be fixed.[4] In that case we can simplify our notation. For example, player i's beliefs concerning the type of player $(1-i)$ and her strategies might be independent of what player i believes about the type of the Jury. In that case the belief of i is the function $\beta_i^\rho : T_i \times \mathcal{H}(\rho) \rightarrow \Delta(T_{1-i}) \times \Delta(S_{(1-i)}^\rho)$. We will simplify the interpretation function similarly.

Let's return to Example (1) to see how types and interpretations might play out in a very simple scenario. Suppose we have two types for 0, roughly one, t_0^g according to which 0 intended to link π_b to π_a via the discourse relation of Result and another type t_0^r

---

[3] Using the definitions of first order beliefs, S, the set of strategies, and types, [5] define higher order beliefs, beliefs that players or the Jury have about the beliefs of other players (and the Jury) and fill out the epistemic picture of our players.

[4] For a definition of independence see [5].

according to which 0 intended to link π_b to π_a via Acknowledgement. Suppose 1 only has one type. In that case, the play ρ_1 together with $\beta_1^\rho : \mathcal{H}(\rho) \to \Delta(T_0)$ determines a probability distribution over the types for 0. In turn these types via $\xi_1^\rho : T_0 \to \Delta(\mathcal{H}(\rho))$ determine a probability distribution over the two histories (2-a) and (2-b) for player 1. [5] shows how such distributions evolve as a conversation proceeds.

4   Analysing Linguistic Bias with ME Games

In what follows, the protests will be the event e, and the messages will select sets of formulas $C_F^t(x)$ to construct histories, depending on the type t of the author.

Media publications through these channels build up a dialogue between conflicting parties with distinct strategies. The recipients are distributed over time and space (not restricted to e.g. a single TV discussion), and there are multiple groups within the recipients. As Fig. 1 shows, the dialogue evolves over time. The quantity of protester contributions (red line) follows an inverse power law with intermittent peaks reflecting the increase of activities during the regular weekend marches, and also some extraordinary events such as the inauguration of Lukashenko on September 23, strikes on October 26, the death of Roman Bondarenko on December 11 (peak from 15/11). The most messages from the opposition come right after the elections and with the first protests, and then gradually die down. Government posts (in blue) stay relatively constant with certain peaks and gradually come to dominate in number the opposition posts. While opposition channels mainly report about protest (selection and coverage bias), state media start reporting about protests after 12 h from their start (selection bias), and allocate in the beginning only a small part of the news to protests (coverage bias).

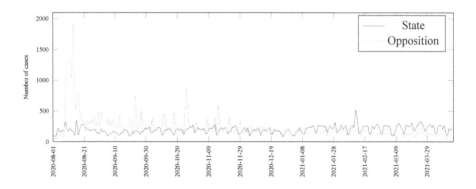

Fig. 1. Dynamics of the conversation (Color figure online)

We analyze this extended conversation as an ME game $\mathcal{G}$ between the protesters (0) and the government (1). Player i constructs a narrative during his turn either about some contemporaneous event or as a reply and "counter-narrative" to player $1 - i$'s narrative on some previous turn. We will consider two types t_0 for PROTESTER and t_1 for the type POLICE, which includes the government controlled media. $\mathcal{G}$ is zero sum;

the winning condition for player i is to convince his readership that her history, which portrays the type t_{1-i} of player $1 - i$ in negative terms, is the correct one. The Jury of this ME game are the interpreters or readers of the posts, either be of type t_0 or t_1, of the contribution. This Jury will assign either favorable or unfavorable ratings to the author's play at a given turn. Player i wins in a game with Jury of type t_j just in case i has more favorable ratings than Player $1 - i$. Figure 1 suggests from the number of posts that arguably player 1 wins G.

We will examine on the strategies that the players use in this game. We focus first on how authors try to invest the type of their opponents with content. We then turn to the dialogue-like structure of this exchange.

4.1 Identities of Protesters and Police

As we have said, authors of each type build quite different histories. Authors of type t will use $C_F^t(x)$ to make plays ρ^t. One of the principal tasks of a history built by t_i is to build a negative identity for the opponent t_{1-i} and indirectly then to paint t_i in a positive light. The identities of the interacting participants are constructed via their own contributions, the contributions of *all* participants *and* the entire interaction history [24]. The aim in these messages for authors of type t_0 is to build sympathy and support for the protesters, and one strategy to do this is to depict the type of opposition as evil— though not always true, the adage, the enemy of evil is good, is an effective strategy. We have seen this strategy already at work in our Examples 1 and 2. Both examples use the word *people* to refer to some social categories. For ONT, *ordinary people* are those who are tired from protests, and protesters are an *aggressive minority*, while for TUT.BY *people* are the protesters. Thus, the category *people* evokes different sets of rights and obligations, and different standartised relationship pairs, depending on the speaker who uses this category. This illustrates how framing or linguistic bias works at the level of membership categorisation.

The post in Example 5 by a player of type t_0, uses a definite description that brings with it a host of associated negative concepts to develop a strategic attack on t_1 (though the use of *punishers* needs some background history to be properly understood).

Example 5. 09.08.2020 20:56 Belsat https://t.me/belsat/10308

*On Masherova Avenue in Minsk, **people** clashed with **OMON**[5]. At least **one of the punishers** had their head smashed.*

The term *punishers* was used to refer to a Nazi division operating in Belarus during the Second World War; the term thus is associated with a number of other concepts [nazi, soldiers, enemy, aggressors, defenders, partisans, army, …]. It associates people of t_1 (via, in MCA terms, the membership-categorization device or MCD) with war, not protests. The historical usage and associations of *punishers* in turn define a characteristic activity of t_1 people: *acting with special cruelty against Belorussian people*. By using *punishers* in the context of the description of a protest, the author of t_0 implies that people of t_1 are waging war against people of t_0. Labelling with terms loaded with

---

[5] Otryad Militsyi Osobogo Nasnacheniya, En.: Special police detachment.

a historical meaning is thought by the authors to be an effective strategy for painting the opponent in negative terms, and to justify the injuries of the police caused by protesters.

Example 6. 09.08.2020 21:06 https://t.me/belsat/10321
*In Mogilev, **cosmonauts** block the streets.*

Attacks by t_i against t_{1-i} do not always use the strategy of depicting t_{1-i} as evil or cruel. In Example 6, the word *cosmonauts* refers to OMON officers wearing their full equipment and helmets, visible in the accompanying photo. The discourse structure of this last example is rather complex as it involves multimodal information. The concept *cosmonauts* evokes a category like space travel and a collection of concepts like [cosmonauts, engineers, scientists, aliens, ...]. The defining property of this class includes *wearing protective clothes and helmets*. This attribute makes them visually similar to OMON police. A certain displacement and ridiculing happens when *cosmonauts* block streets in Mogilev (far away from any space-travel area). This is also an effective strategy to promote t_0, the type of the protesters. By ridiculing the opposition t_1, the author puts t_0 in a position of authority and *gravitas*. Both *punishers* in Example 5 and *cosmonauts* in Example 6 are marked: *punishers* with anger and fear, and *cosmonauts* with displacement.

The government information sites also use various labeling strategies to characterize their opponents in negative terms. State channels report events in the night from 9th to 10th August (bold added by us) as follows.

Example 7. 10.08.2020 10:57 ONT https://t.me/pressmvd/1890
*On the night of 9 to 10 August 2020, **Focal gatherings of citizens**... were recorded in the country.*
*In total, about 3 thousand **people** were detained throughout the country for participating in **unauthorized mass events**... As a result of the **clashes**, more than 50 **citizens** were injured, as well as 39 **police officers**, some of whom are currently hospitalized.*
*In Minsk at 22.00 in the area of the stele "Minsk - Hero City", **protesters** lit fireworks, threw spikes and nails on the roadway, erected barricades from mobile turnstiles, dismantled paving slabs and threw them and other objects at **law enforcement officers**.*
*An active resistance to the **law enforcement bodies** was rendered in Pinsk, where a **group of aggressively minded citizens**, using pointed stakes, rods, stones and reinforcement bars, tried to organize an attack on **police officers**. **Some of the citizens** taken to the country's medical institutions were in a **state of alcoholic intoxication**.*
*! It should be noted that military weapons were not used against **violators**. There are no fatalities.*

The news channel ONT refers to the protests first as *focal gatherings* and *unauthorized mass events*. Crucially no mention is made of why the protesters are gathering. The category *protesters* is used in the third paragraph of the news bulletin, but it assigns to them rather violent properties against *police officers* and *law enforcement bodies*. All in all the protesters are painted in a negative light, which justifies the actions of the police.

Example 8. 10.08.2020 11:54 BelTA https://youtu.be/BjS1uHqbRaY

Video: *We detained the **organizers** who were **hiding** and **running around the corner**. About three thousand - half of them in Minsk - **stoned**, Sergei Nikolaevich*[6], *there are **many drunks**, **with drugs**, horror.*

The President of Belarus on the same day describes the events in Example 8 and then two days later introduces a new theme (Example 9).

Example 9. 12.08.2020 14:24 Pool 1, https://t.me/pul_1/1250 *Lukashenka: "The basis of all these **so-called protesters** are **people with a criminal past** and are **unemployed** today". There is no job, which means they can "walk the streets and avenues".*

Examples 8 and 9 characterize protesters as unemployed alcoholics, addicts and criminals. What is used as an occasional feature in Example 7 (*being in a state of alcoholic intoxication*) becomes at least a tight feature in Example 8 (*stoned, many drunks, with drugs*). Example 9 uses the description of activity *walk the streets and avenues* as a justification of the presence of people on the streets. This activity in turn, is a consequence of the people's unemployment. The marker *so-called* modifies *protesters* giving it an ironic or sarcastic reading *distancing* its meaning on this occasion from its normal one [15]. Table 1 summarizes the way t_0 and t_1 are characterized.

Table 1. Labeling of *protesters* and *police* by opposition and state channels.

Types	By t_0 (protesters)	By t_1 (police)
t_0 (**protesters**)	People, protesters	People, citizens, protesters, violators, so-called protesters, people with criminal past, unemployed, sheep, drunks
Attributes		Stoned, drunk, with drugs, people with criminal past, unemployed, aggressively minded, in a state of alcoholic intoxication
Actions	Gather in the center of Minsk, clash with OMON, smash heads of OMON, build barricades, throw bottles at OMON, break through the cordons	Lit fires, threw spikes and nails on the roadway, built barricades, dismantled paving slabs and threw them and other objects at police, attack police officers, use pointed stakes, rods, stones and reinforcement bars, hiding, running around the corner, are being controlled, do not understand what they are doing
t_1 (**police**)	Riot police, OMON, punishers, cosmonauts	Law enforcement bodies, law enforcement officers, police officers
Actions	Clash with protesters, use flash bangs, block streets	Did not use military weapons, detain organisers

To sum up, different news channels use different labelling strategies, picking out different defining features for our types, to get complex messages across.

---

[6] Lebedev, Executive Secretary of the CIS.

4.2 The "Neutral" View Point

As shown in Sect. 3, a play may develop different histories depending on the type of the interpreter (see discussion of Example 4). Thus, the histories h^{I_0} and h^{I_1} constructed by interpreters of the two types may also differ, even though they both arise from the interpretation a single play ρ, as in Example 10:

Example 10. 09.08.2020 20:11 Belsat https://t.me/belsat/10272

*About **20–30 locals**, including **children**, gathered in the park on Hrybaedava Street (Minsk) near Stella. Two **paddy wagons** came to the park, **police officers** said that **people** had 2 min to **go away**, after which they started to **push people out of the park**. A Belsat correspondent witnessed how one **person** was detained but later **released**. After trying to **evict people from the park**, the **paddy wagons left** and the **people returned** to the park. There are 3 ambulances on duty, near to them **people in plainclothes** are standing.*

Example 10 labels persons as *locals* and *children*. The action attributed to them *gathered in the park* together with these labels evoke a scene of leisure activity in which parents and children are going to the park (some of those people were with children, they must be parents to those children)—which all sounds innocuous.

The narrative then changes as *paddy wagons* and *police officers* enter the scene and the actions now contrast with the scene of leisure activity evoked above. The police arguably confront the people by saying *that people had 2 min to go away* and then by starting to *push out people of the park*. These events need to be related to the gathering in a coherent history, but the author does not explicitly say why the paddy wagons arrived or the police acted in this way. The police actions towards *locals, children and people* arguably cause us to interpret a *gathering in the park* as an undesired event.

At this point an interpreter has two interpretive strategies with two distinct semantic relations relating the sentence contents: (1) The gathering was illegal and hence the actions of the police are a natural and legitimate Result; OR (2) The gathering is legal and in Contrast the police are acting in a wrong way.

These readings depend on the readers' prior beliefs and political preferences. Government supporters would read it as "police prevented escalation", opposition supporters would read it as "government uses power for oppression". This example shows how interpreters or readers contribute to a biased reading by inferring semantic relations between discourse units to form a coherent narrative.

The last sentence then introduces *people in plainclothes* which are arguably not the same as *locals* or just *people*, although *locals* usually wear plainclothes. The attribute *plainclothes* refers to the appearance of people who are supposed to wear something different but wear plainclothes, probably in order to hide their identity. Again depending on the type of the interpreter, this second paragraph has two messages: (1) a reassurance: police officers are still there, protecting law and order; OR (2) a warning: if you go to this park, you might by observed by the *people in plainclothes* or even *detained*.

Example 11. 09.08.2020 21:04 Belsat https://t.me/belsat/10317

*In the center of Minsk **OMON** uses flash bangs against **protesters**.*

Even messages that use only unmarked references to police and protesters, such as Example 11, will be colored by the reader's bias in a positive or negative way.

4.3 Interaction Between Protester and Police

We have examined strategies by the players in our game that are used on individual turns to convince their readership. Here we detail strategies for player i's replies to previous turns by $1 - i$. Player 1 Police plays the move from Example 12:

Example 12. 10.08.2020 13:24 ONT t.me/ontnews/13864
*We identified calls from abroad. The calls came from Poland, UK and Czech Republic, they controlled our - excuse me - **sheep**: they do not understand what they are doing, and they are being controlled.*

In response, player 0 Protester plays the move as illustrated in Example 13, in which a photo of a person holding a piece of white cardboard with text written on it in red letters conveys the message that protesters reject the attributes, such as *unemployed* and *sheep*, assigned to them by an author of type t_1 in the previous message. The visual is an effective strategy; rather than the author verbally rejecting the negative labels provided by player 1 of type t_1, it is a winsome, smiling protester who is conveying the message rejecting the government's labelling strategy. In addition, she is using the symbolic colors of the opposition (red and white) to do it.

Example 13. 13.08.20 13:37 Belarus Sejchas https://t.me/belarusseichas/5827

Today in Minsk.

Text on the picture:
We are not sheep, we have jobs.

Another strategy by player 0 to attack the histories proposed by 1 is to point out inconsistencies and contradictions. Example 14 illustrates this. Part of 1's strategy is to attack the identity of player 0 via attributes not related to political content such as employment, alcohol consumption, bad parenting, and affiliation to particular profession. But this conflicts with other labelling strategies.

Example 14. Belsat 12.01.2021 12:26 https://t.me/belsat/38767
Video: *"The basis of this **protest** is made up of **these IT people** who are **snickering**, excuse me, **who were nearly kissed the ass**…"*
Text: *Wait, but some **alcoholics**, **drug addicts** and **parasites** come out to protest. Apparently, **state television** is finally **confused** in its own versions.*

Examples 12, 13 and 14 show that messages produced by the prototypical speaker of the type Police build first pair parts, and responses produces by the prototypical speaker of the type Protester build second pair parts. Although these first and second parts are not adjacent in terms of face-to-face conversation, they analysably form adjacency pairs. While the Protester frequently responds to the Police's messages in our dataset, we found only few adjacency pairs in which the Protester produced the first, and the Police the second pair part.

4.4 Dynamics and Bias Hardening

Asher et al. [3] use the model explained in Sect. 3 to predict that interpreters' biases become more entrenched through the co-dependence of belief and interpretation: prior beliefs or the distribution over types will guide I to a particular interpretation. In turn, that interpretation can reinforce those initial beliefs over time. We see empirical evidence of bias hardening in the corpus.

One strategy is to appropriate a label from an opponent and reassign it in negative connotations. For example, opposition channels use the label 'unbelievable' as adjective to emphasize the bravery of the Belorussian protesters: https://t.me/belarusseichas/7388 from 14/08/2020 shows a video of a peaceful demonstration with the text "*Unbelievable people*". State channels, however, then re-use this to label protesters 'the unbelievables' and to link it with actions described as meaningless or aggressive (Example 15).

Example 15. ONT 19.10.2020 18:37 https://t.me/ontnews/19205

Protests of the 'fighters' have long ceased to be peaceful. The participants intentionally take to the streets and provoke ordinary citizens, throwing themselves with aggression at those who do not agree with their views. The footage shows the unbelievables starting fights and doing everything they can to heat up the situation in society.

Over time, *the unbelievables* becomes synonymous with *pointless aggressive protests* and is used alone without further explanations. Figure 2 shows the successful appropriation of the term *unbelievable* by state media.

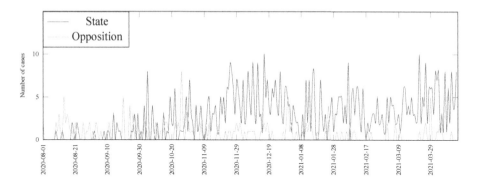

Fig. 2. State takes up the use of 'unbelievable' to label protesters

These examples show the non-cooperative nature of the dialogue between state and opposition players. Participants do not co-construct meaning; rather, they present different versions of meaning to the readership or Jury, typed as POLICE and PROTESTER. We showed in Sect. 4.1 how selective formulations create different identities of protesters and police. The sequential organisation of those selective formulations results in different interpretations of entire conversations.

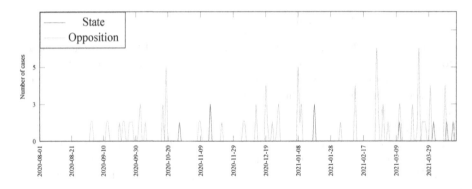

Fig. 3. Opposition takes up the use of 'yabatska' to label state supporters

Example 16. Belarus Seychas 17.10.2020 15:03 https://t.me/belarusseichas/13064
    This is nothing new. It's just that the yabatskas stipulate the amount they get for participation in pro-Lukashenko events

Similarly, the opposition successfully appropriates the term *yabatska* which is a composite of *ya-mi-batskka, En.: me-us-father*. Originally used to express solidarity with the president (e.g., https://t.me/belta_telegramm/15842), the term taken up by the opposition media to describe state supporters as uncultivated, uninformed and unable to think critically (Example 16). Figure 3 shows how the opposition appropriated the label *yabatska*.

5   Discussion and Conclusions

Our corpus confirms [16] observations concerning *gatekeeping* or *selection* bias (the choice of a channel to report an issue or not), *coverage* bias (how much space in the media is dedicated to an event) and *framing* bias (the way a fact is presented). Our model, however, sharpens the notions of framing and coverage biases by linking them to strategies at the lexical and discursive level that can be opportunistic and evolve over time. We also see the confirmation of different levels of bias granularity in our corpus: category-level, message-level and media source level [2, 8]: The examples discussed in Sect. 4.1 illustrate how choices of marked categories (*punishers, cosmonauts*) create biased identities. Examples in Sect. 2 illustrate how message-level bias is implemented by selective reporting (stun grenades vs. blocked entrances) and selective formulations (*people* vs. *aggressive minorities*). We discussed how entire channels are biased in the beginning of Sect. 4, Fig. 1.

   In addition, our game theoretic model captures the important role of the recipient/interpreter of messages, even when those are neutrally formulated. We have shown how different histories arise from different although valid interpretations of the same message. In contrast to previous bias-detection work based on static models [10, 19], our model is able to deal with dynamics in linguistic bias. We explained how biases can harden into established opinion and exploit strategies for appropriating terms from an opponent for one's own discourse purposes. In line with [7], we have shown these discourse purposes can encode normative reasoning and specific rationales for physical harm and restrictions of freedoms of the opponents. Our qualitative study shows that complex historical background and values of the target recipients, which we can express as types in our model, play an important role in bias construction and detection. None of the existing static models is able to capture these factors. Embedding-based approaches may be helpful to find collocations and discover asymmetries based on word choice even for an unknown set of labels [10], however, they cannot discover omitted facts or details, nor are they able to express the dynamics of the conversation. The training corpora used for any machine-learning approach only provide a snapshot view on the histories, and the models need to be continuously retrained on new data in order to learn new labels. The opportunistic nature of labelling, as explained in Sect. 4.4, questions lexicon and embedding-based approaches. In addition, seemingly neutral labels (such as *people* vs. *ordinary people* vs. *people in plainclothes*) are usually not considered as potentially biased, especially in lexicon-based approaches, such as [2].

Finally, our study issues a challenge to automated de-biasing of political news. A completely neutral viewpoint does not exist. If it were to exist, it should be non-selective in terms of issues to report (what is important enough to be reported?), equally covering (all parties must have access to all channels equally), and non-selective in terms of formulations (lexical choice) and details (how complete is the picture?). Examples in Sect. 4.1 illustrate this finding.

This study has empirical limitations: we analysed only one political event in only one country. Although we understand the import of the cultural context, more comparison is needed with other events of a similar controversial degree, e.g. Navalny protests in Russia, the US Black Lives Matter movement, anti-Corona restrictions movement (mis)used by right radicals and protests in Hong-Kong, just to name a few. Analyzing such data is also technically difficult. Messengers like Telegram typically become the main source of communication in many political conflicts. They galvanize public opinion and can move masses of people in real time. However, messages with photos and videos pose challenges to computational analysis beyond those from newspaper articles.

References

1. Akbari, A., Gabdulhakov, R.: Platform surveillance and resistance in Iran and Russia: the case of Telegram. Surveill. Soc. **17**(1/2), 223–231 (2019)
2. Aleksandrova, D., Lareau, F., Ménard, P.A.: Multilingual sentence-level bias detection in Wikipedia. In: Proceedings International Conference on Recent Advances in Natural Language Processing (RANLP 2019), Varna, Bulgaria, pp. 42–51 (2019)
3. Asher, N., Hunter, J., Paul, S.: Bias in semantic and discourse interpretation. Linguist. Philos. 1–37 (2021). https://doi.org/10.1007/s10988-021-09334-x
4. Asher, N., Lascarides, A.: Logics of Conversation. Cambridge University Press, Cambridge (2003)
5. Asher, N., Paul, S.: Strategic conversations under imperfect information: epistemic message exchange games. J. Logic Lang. Inform. **27**(4), 343–385 (2018)
6. Beukeboom, C.J., Burgers, C.: Linguistic bias. In: Oxford Research Encyclopedia, Communication. Oxford University Press (2020)

7. Blodgett, S.L., Barocas, S., Daumé III, H., Wallach, H.: Language (technology) is power: a critical survey of "bias" in NLP. In: Proceedings of the 58th ACL Meeting, pp. 5454–5476. ACL (2020)
8. Chen, W.F., Al-Khatib, K., Wachsmuth, H., Stein, B.: Analyzing political bias and unfairness in news articles at different levels of granularity. arXiv preprint arXiv:2010.10652 (2020)
9. Kvetkin, P.D.: Russian tiktok: a space not free from politics. In: MEDIAObrazovaniye: Media kak Totalnaya Povsednevnost, pp. 370–374 (2020)
10. Ferrer Aran, X., van Nuenen, T., Such, J., Criado Pacheco, N.: Discovering and categorising language biases in Reddit. In: Proceedings of the 15th International AAAI Conference on Web and Social Media (ICWSM 2021), pp. 140–151 (2021)
11. Fischer, K.: Designing Speech for a Recipient: The Roles of Partner Modeling, Alignment and Feedback in So-Called 'Simplified Registers', vol. 270. John Benjamins Publishing Company (2016)
12. Freiberg, J., Freebody, P.: Applying membership categorisation analysis to discourse: when the 'tripwire critique' is not enough. In: Le, T., Le, Q., Short, M. (eds.) Critical Discourse Analysis: An Interdisciplinary Perspective, pp. 49–64. Nova Science Publishers (2009)
13. Gibson, W., Roca-Cuberes, C.: Constructing blame for school exclusion in an online comments forum: membership categorisation analysis and endogenous category work. Discourse Context Media 32, 100331 (2019)
14. Harsanyi, J.C.: Games with incomplete information played by "Bayesian" players, I–III Part I. The basic model. Manag. Sci. 14(3), 159–182 (1967)
15. Härtl, H.: Name-informing and distancing sogenannt 'so-called': name mentioning and the lexicon-pragmatics interface. Z. Sprachwiss. 37(2), 139–169 (2018)
16. Lazaridou, K., Krestel, R.: Identifying political bias in news articles. Bull. IEEE Tech. Comm. Digit. Libr. 12 (2016)
17. McLay, K.F.: Geeks, gamers, and girls: revealing diverse digital identities with membership categorisation analysis. Discourse Stud. Cult. Polit. Educ. 40(6), 946–961 (2019)
18. Philo, G.: Political advertising and popular belief. In: The Glasgow Media Group Reader, vol. II: Industry, Economy, War and Politics, pp. 184–197 (1995)
19. Reddy, R.R., Duggenpudi, S.R., Mamidi, R.: Detecting political bias in news articles using headline attention. In: Proceedings of the 2019 ACL Workshop BlackboxNLP: Analyzing and Interpreting Neural Networks for NLP, Florence, Italy, pp. 77–84. Association for Computational Linguistics (2019)
20. Sacks, H.: On the analyzability of stories by children. In: Directions in Sociolinguistics. The Ethnography of Communications, pp. 325–345. Holt, Rinehart and Winston (1972)
21. Sacks, H.: Lectures on Conversation, vol. 1 and 2. Blackwell (1995)
22. Schegloff, E.A.: Sequence Organization in Interaction: Volume 1: A Primer in Conversation Analysis. Cambridge University Press (2007)
23. Schegloff, E.A.: A tutorial on membership categorization. J. Pragmat. 39(3), 462–482 (2007)
24. Spranz-Fogasy, T.: Interaktionsprofile: Die Herausbildung individueller Handlungstypik in Gesprächen. Verlag für Gesprächsforschung, Radolfzell (2002)
25. Stivers, T.: Sequence organization. In: Sidnell, J., Stivers, T. (eds.) The Handbook of Conversation Analysis, chap. 10, pp. 191–209. Wiley (2012)

Identifying Topical Shifts in Twitter Streams: An Integration of Non-negative Matrix Factorisation, Sentiment Analysis and Structural Break Models for Large Scale Data

Mattias Luber[1], Christoph Weisser[1,2](✉), Benjamin Säfken[1,2], Alexander Silbersdorff[1,2], Thomas Kneib[1,2], and Krisztina Kis-Katos[1,2]

[1] Georg-August-Universität Göttingen, Göttingen, Germany
christoph.weisser@oxon.org
[2] Campus-Institut Data Science (CIDAS), Göttingen, Germany

Abstract. We propose an integration of Non-negative Matrix Factorisation, Sentiment analysis and Structural Break Models to identify significant topical shifts on the social media platform Twitter. For the topic modelling, we compare Latent Dirichlet Allocation and Non-negative Matrix Factorization in terms of their applicability to short text documents. The extraction of sentiment is done by the rule-based VADER model. Structural breaks in the relative frequency and daily sentiments of topics over time are identified with the Bai-Perron model. Combining these methods, we provide a valuable and easy to use exploratory tool for social scientists to study the discourse on Twitter over time. Detecting statistically significant shifts in topics over time enables researchers to perform statistical inference and test hypotheses about the discourse on Twitter. The framework is implemented efficiently to ensure that it can be used on average consumer hardware in a reasonable amount of time. A case study with COVID-19 related tweets in the UK is provided. Our method is validated by linking the topical shifts to real world events by the use of the timestamps of the COVID-19 related tweets.

Keywords: Twitter · Social media · Topic model · Non-negative Matrix Factorisation · Sentiment analysis · Structural Break Models

1 Introduction

For research in the social sciences, the content of discussions on social media and on micro-blogs such as Twitter are highly relevant as they allow to capture shifts in public sentiment and discourse. We provide a user-friendly framework to model the discourse on Twitter by applying natural language processing methods to user-generated Twitter data. We compare Latent Dirichlet Allocation (LDA) [7]

J. Bright et al. (Eds.): MISDOOM 2021, LNCS 12887, pp. 33–49, 2021.
https://doi.org/10.1007/978-3-030-87031-7_3

and Non-negative Matrix Factorization (NMF) [9, 19] in terms of their applicability to short text documents and find that the NMF leads to substantially better results. Sentiments are extracted with the rule-based VADER model [12] and shifts in the topical prevalence are identified endogenously with the Bai-Perron model [6]. We provide efficient implementations to ensure that our framework can be used on average consumer hardware in a reasonable amount of time. By combining these methods, we provide a tool for social scientist to study the discourse on Twitter over time. In particular, our approach allows users to detect statistically significant shifts in the discourse of topics.

Our framework is tested in a case study relying on COVID-19 related tweets in the UK. We identify topics that are linked to the context of COVID-19, determine their sentiment, and model their development over time. The results are validated by linking the topical shifts to real world events by the use of the timestamps of the COVID-19 related tweets.

The remainder of the paper is structured as follows. Section 2 discusses related work. Section 3.1 outlines the data collection and pre-processing. Since the data is streamed directly from Twitter, there are specific requirements to be met to enable a time efficient analysis with average consumer hardware. Section 3.2 introduces the sentiment analysis with the VADER model. The estimation of topics models and a comparison of the LDA and NMF is provided in Sect. 3.3. Section 4.3 outlines the Bai-Perron model. Results are presented and linked to real word events in Sect. 4. Section 5 discusses and concludes and provides suggestions for further research.

2   Related Work

Sentiment analysis in general is a well researched topic across multiple domains, but especially in context of social media data and micro-blogs. The proposed methods are quite diverse and range from lexicon-based, over rule-based approaches up to complex deep neural networks [22]. An extensive overview and comparison of different methodologies in particular for Twitter data can be found in [11] or [33].

For topic modelling, several NMF [9, 19]- or LDA [7]-based approaches exists. However, not all of them are directly applicable for micro-blog data because of the specific challenges of short and sparse text. There are extensions that take these into account and it has been shown that this can indeed improve the estimates [29]. Despite its potential limitations, we build our framework on the basic configuration of NMF since it provides good results and furthermore is well-researched, robust, and intuitive to understand. More details on this decision can be found in the methodology section. A probabilistic alternative for short text would be the Dirichlet Multinomial Model [28].

On the framework level, current approaches are still often either build heuristically or require manual annotations, especially in the context of socioeconomic analysis. PoliTwi [20] as an example narrows down the concept of topics to single hashtags and then tries to track emerging political topics by simply visualizing their occurrence over time. In a similar manner, Adedoyin-Olowe et al. [1] use automated rule mining to detect events through trending hashtags. Yaqub et al. [27] associate keywords with sentiment scores to gather insight about the US elections 2016. Cases where manual annotations are required [33] are problematic as Twitter data is usually unlabeled and the process of labeling is generally extremely time consuming and not scalable.

Nevertheless, it also has been shown that the connection of sentiment analysis and topic modelling can provide valuable insights for better understanding the discussion on social media [2,4,18] and that topic models can be used to trace the change of events [26,32]. We extend those insights by applying the Bai-Perron model [5,6] for detecting structural changes in the topics discussed on Twitter. The Bai-Perron model is specifically designed to identify multiple structural breaks in a time series, without a-priori information about the break point. Thereby we can not only detect the presence of an event or change points in sentiment, but also provide statistical confidence intervals for their time-points.

In a broader context the modelling of the Twitter discourse is a quite diverse field, which also includes fundamentally different approaches like frame detection [13], network analysis [25] or evaluation of disinformation campaigns[14]. An overview about the current literature on Twitter analysis can be found in Antonakaki et al. [3].

3   Methodology

An overview of the framework is provided in Fig. 1. After collecting tweets via the Twitter-API, the data are pre-processed such that hyperlinks and mentions are removed and the texts were set to lowercase. After that, the workflow splits into two major branches, which are topic modelling and sentiment analysis. Topic modelling is used to identify the most influential topics that are discussed on Twitter and delivers word-clouds for each of them. In parallel to that, the sentiment analysis annotates each tweet with a sentiment score. These two types of outcomes are aggregated into a time-series of daily relative frequencies of topics and their average daily sentiment, Finally, the structural break models are run on each topic separately to detect statistically significant shifts in their frequency and the related sentiments. Finally, the user is provided with valuable information about the topics, their occurrence, as well as with time-points of structural breaks in the frequency of topics as well as in topic-specific sentiment. Each component is explained in more detail in the following sections.

3.1   Data Collection and Preprocessing

The data was collected with the Twitter API in the time period between 25th October 2020 and 14th January 2021 with the python package Tweepy [21] and a geo-location filter for the United Kingdom. Tweepy connects to the Twitter sample stream, which provides access to a random 1% subsample of all tweets published in the given area in real time. At the time point of data collection,

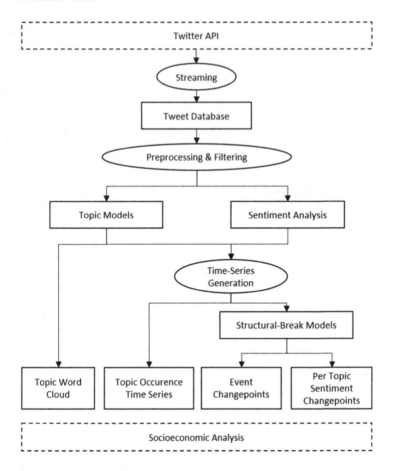

Fig. 1. Visualization of the overall workflow of our framework

no additional filters were applied to ensure that the data is as complete and unbiased as possible. The tweets were accessed as they were published. This was explicitly intended to ensure that later deletions or modifications of tweets would not affect the analysis.

One key difference between the study of Twitter data and classical text mining is that the documents can have fundamentally different properties that have to be taken into account. Users on social media platforms often use a distinct vocabulary that contains more slang, emojis, and hashtags than standard language does. Furthermore, especially on micro-blogs like Twitter, the documents tend to be extremely short.

This gives rise to new challenges as most of the algorithms for text analysis were designed for classical documents and are not guaranteed to work on nonstandard language. To compensate for that, only 'extended tweets' were included in the analysis, which are at least 160 characters long. In addition, retweets and replies were excluded to get the true user-generated content only.

After data collection, a lexicon-based filtering is applied to extract the share of tweets that are associated with COVID-19. Only posts are included that contain at least one word of the lexicon in Fig. 2. The lexicon is designed heuristically by identifying words and hashtags that are often used in the context of the COVID-19 pandemic. It contains words and hashtags that are expected to be used neutrally, but also most exclusively within the context of the pandemic. For instance, words like "stay" and "safe" would not be good choices because they are too generic while the hashtag 'staysafe' is nowadays almost exclusively used in association with COVID-19 and can as such be used for filtering. After pre-processing and applying the filtering procedure, about 71.000 COVID-19 related tweets remain. This is about 10% of the original data.

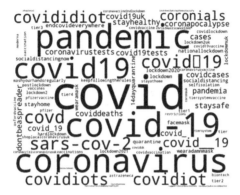

Fig. 2. A wordcloud of the lexicon, which was used for filtering COVID-19 related tweets.

3.2 Sentiment Analysis

The streamed data does not contain true sentiment labels, so that supervised machine learning based models cannot be used. Instead, we implement the rule-based VADER model [12]. The outcome of the prediction is a compound score, ranging on a continuous scale from the most negative (-1) over neutral (0) to the most positive (1).

VADER works with lists of positive and negative words, but in contrast to other rule-based models, it also takes basic grammatical and syntactical features into account. For example, some amplifying words like "very" or "extremely" would not change the sentiment, but increase its intensity. "But" on the other hand, is used to detect sentiment changes. Here the weights of preceding words are lowered while the upcoming words are amplified. The biggest advantage of VADER is probably, that it is designed with social media applications in mind and hence it can deal with common slang phrases and emoticons. Moreover, it does not require any training steps and despite its simplicity, it scores surprisingly well across various domains. The original paper states that correlations up to 0.88 with user ratings could be observed and in a self-conducted evaluation on the SemEval2018 dataset [17] of labeled tweets a correlation of round about 0.7 is reached. This is indeed in a similar range of the more complex models, which score between 0.7 and 0.8.

Sentiment in the context of this analysis does not necessarily reflect the opinion towards a certain topic. It rather gives an indication if the discussion about a certain topic has heated up or is loaded with strong positive or negative emotions.

3.3 Topic Modelling

Topic modelling describes the extraction of underlying topics as hidden semantic structures in text documents. Two algorithms, which are often recommended for this tasks, are Latent Dirichlet Allocation (LDA) [7] and Non-negative-Matrix-Factorization (NMF) [9,19]. Both work with a Bag-of-Words representation of documents, which means that a document is fully defined by its words, while the semantic structure is neglected. LDA models topics as hidden variables and follows a probabilistic approach. By contrast, NMF is essentially a matrix factorization that tries to minimize a reconstruction error.

In the following, the applicability of both algorithms is briefly outlined with particular attention to the special characteristics of micro-blogs and tweets. Since the NMF turned out to work better for the analysis of COVID-19 related tweets, the further evaluation is carried out with this model only.

Latent Dirichlet Allocation. For topic modelling, LDA is often considered the established state of the art since it yields good results and furthermore comes with an implicit measure of uncertainty due to its probabilistic perspective. LDA assumes a data generating process, where each document can be described by a distribution over k latent topics, and each topic is a distribution over the vocabulary. New documents are then generated by repeatedly drawing a topic first and then sampling a word from its distribution.

While LDA performs well on longer texts it shows shortcomings on short and sparse documents such as tweets. Chen et al. [29] conducted a comprehensive exploratory study for various topic modelling algorithms and find that LDA indeed leads to worse results for short and spare text. A reason is the extremely sparse document-feature matrices for short and spare text which makes word-word co-occurrences harder to estimate. Especially for the probabilistic approach this compromises the ability of the model to capture the underlying structure since the estimates are affected by a high variance [29]. Furthermore, one key assumption of LDA is that each document can contain more then one topic. However, due to the short and sparse nature of tweets, it is reasonable to suppose that they are mostly mono-thematic.

To overcome the sparsity, various pooling procedures are proposed, where several tweets are aggregated into pseudo-documents, e.g., based on their hashtags [16]. Within our analysis, such a hashtag-pooling would interfere with the chosen filtering approach since tweets are collected based on certain hashtags like "covid19" or "coronavirus".

Those hashtags occur in a substantial amount of posts. If hashtags are then used for the aggregation, some extremely large documents are created, while the vast majority is still very short. Besides the highly skewed document length, this results in an unnaturally imbalanced number of topics per document since general purpose hashtags are used with basically every subtopic, while really specific ones are still mono-thematic.

Non-negative-Matrix-Factorization. NMF treats topic modelling as a matrix factorization problem. It approximates the data matrix of observed documents X as the product of a coefficient matrix W and a component matrix H, i.e., $X \approx W * H$. The matrices W and H are derived by minimizing the reconstruction error in respect to the Frobenius norm with the additional constraint that all coefficients have to be non-negative. Documents are hence modelled as linear combinations of the components, and due to the non-negativity of the coefficients, the components become interpretable as topics.

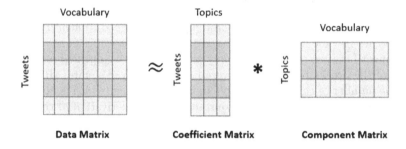

Fig. 3. Top-level visualization of the Non-negative Matrix Factorization algorithm.

Note that NMF also makes the assumption that tweets can contain a mixture of topics. However, we find that NMF performs substantially better than LDA in terms of the extreme sparsity of short mono-thematic documents, since it can be initialized with sparse components [8] and has clustering properties [10,15].

3.4 Time Series Generation

By default, topic coefficients as well as sentiment scores are defined on the level of individual tweets.

To calculate a metric that measures the daily prevalence of a topic over time, all rows from the coefficient matrix of the NMF are normalized, (with the sum of the coefficients in a row) such that the coefficients add up to 1. This makes the scoring comparable between different tweets. After that, a post is said to contain a sufficient amount of a topic i if the corresponding coefficient exceeds a threshold of 0.3. For each topic, the coefficients that fulfill this criterion are aggregated per day to show at which times a certain topic was mostly discussed. Setting this threshold can help to improve the signal in the daily topic prevalence. This is because after the normalization, tweets which can not be assigned to any topic at all end up with approximately uniformly distributed coefficients across all topics. Aggregating coefficients without filtering would therefore lead to a high noise ratio in the time-series caused by unassigned tweets.

This approach was chosen in accordance to the assumptions made by the NMF algorithm, which explicitly allows a document to contain more the one topic. As an example, if any tweet consists of two topics in equal shares, it now contributes to both related topic time series in that ratio. A totally mono-thematic post would respectively contribute to its time series with its full coefficient.

The sentiment scores are binned into "negative", "neutral" and "positive" and here the fraction of negative tweets within each day is used as a time-series. The series are once derived globally across all tweets and in addition for each topic separately.

3.5   Structural Break Models

The structural break model by Bai-Peron [6] was developed to identify multiple change-points in time series data. The general idea is to fit a linear model for each segment between two change-points and to derive the optimal number and location of the breaks based on the overall residual sum of squares (RSS). Even if the true number of changes would be known in advance (which is not the case in most applications and also not in our analysis) the derivation of the optimal placement would still be computationally expensive, since m breaks and n time-points imply $\binom{n}{k}$ possible combinations. For an unknown number of break-points this gets even more problematic. As a solution the estimation is done by the help of dynamic programming to ensure an efficient implementation [31].

Since this model is essentially approximating the time series by piecewise linear functions, additional breakpoints would always lead to an improvement of the total RSS. To compensate for that, the optimal number of break-points are determined via the Bayesian Information Criterion (BIC) which penalizes additional model complexity. As a result a new break is only introduced, if it is justified by an sufficient improvement in terms of RSS [30].

One of the biggest advantages of the Bai-Peron model is that each break-point comes with a statistical confidence interval, which allows a quantification of the uncertainty and hypothesis testing. Furthermore, as the segments between two breakpoints can be interpreted as linear models, the slope and intercept coefficients can be used to quantify the impact and development of structural changes [5].

4   Application on COVID-19 Related Tweets

Since the outbreak of COVID-19 in early 2020, the pandemic has certainly been one of the major topics in almost every aspect of life, but it especially affected public opinion and discourse on healthcare, politics and society. While the effect of measures and restrictions on the spread of the virus can be more or less directly assessed by analysing changes in the number of reported infections, the public perceptions of those measures are harder to capture directly.

Our framework can help to measure the topic-specific public opinion in Twitter data and help to assess the public acceptance if certain policy measures. This is relevant not only for socioeconomic research purposes, but also for pandemic monitoring as acceptance matters for behaviour [23,24].

4.1   Encoding Sentiment

The sentiment for each tweet is predicted with VADER and the resulting compound scores are binned into three classes. Scores between $[-1, -0.3)$ are classified as negative, $[-0.3, 0.3]$ as neutral and $(0.3, 1]$ as positive. Then the fractions of negative as well as positive tweets are calculated per day and tracked over time to visualize how the sentiment developed.

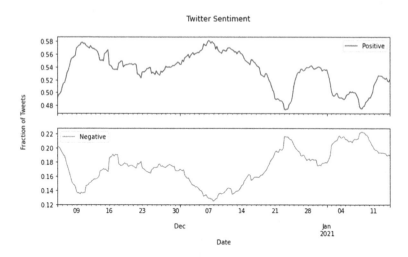

Fig. 4. The fraction of negative and positive Covid-related tweets per day. Especially during December a strong increase in negativity can be observed.

4.2   Establishing Topics

The evaluation of the NMF-based topic model was primarily done by plotting word-clouds of the highest scoring words per topic of the component matrix of the NMF. Twitter is used for commercial purposes to a great extent, and despite the filtering, still quite a lot of advertisements were contained in the data. However, those clustered together in shopping related topics and did not impair the quality of the topics of interest. Some of the identified topics are clearly related to COVID-19, such as the topics "lockdown", "vaccine" or "tier system" as shown in Fig. 5, others reflected some general events that took place during that time, like e.g. New Years Eve and Christmas.

Fig. 5. Selected NMF-topics visualized as wordclouds. Some of them are clearly event related, while others reflect a more continuous discussion about e.g. restrictions in context of COVID-19.

Figure 6 reveals that different topics hold different characteristics. While some are clearly event related and mainly discussed around certain time points, others reflect a more continuous discussion. In context of the evaluation, the time series visualization can be used as a consistency check for the topic model results. In general, the evaluation of topic models is not trivial, since no such thing as a ground truth exists. However, in this case we know the major historical events during the investigated time period. If events can be clearly linked to topics that are related to those events, this shows that the discussion actually indeed centered around those events. For example, if the "New Year" topic would have been discussed at any other time-point then the actual New Year's Eve, it would be highly questionable that the model actually captured the real life concept behind it. For the topics on "Vaccine", "Lockdown" and "Tier System", this evaluation is done in detail in Sect. 4.3 in combination with Bai-Perron models that are used to detect events and structural breaks.

4.3 Event Detection with Structural Break Models

To formalize the process of event detection in the generated time series, the Bai-Perron model is applied with a relatively small trimming factor of 0.05. Thus,

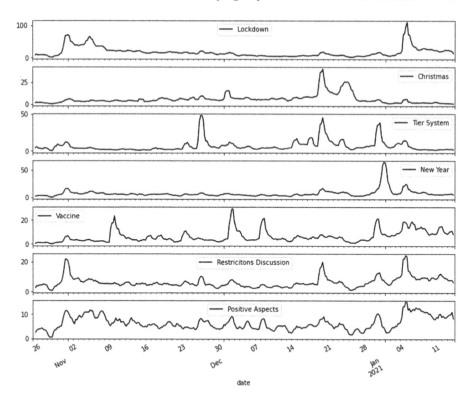

Fig. 6. The occurrence of some selected topics along the timeline. The occurrence is measured by the number of tweets, which had a corresponding normalized coefficient of at least 0.3. The y-axis reflects the summed coefficients per topic for those tweets within a six hour window and is smoothed over a day.

the model is able to frame event-related peaks quite closely and therefore yields good results in regard to their detection.

For the evaluation of the event detection, the breakpoints are of special interest. As mentioned, an in depth investigation is done for the "Vaccine", "Lockdown" and "Tier System" topics, since here the major real-world events during that time are well captured by classical media sources and therefore can be verified.

The complete comparison is listed in the following table. The results show, that indeed for the topics and break-points a clear linkage to a corresponding real-world event can be drawn. For the "Lockdown" topic, the events are centered around the announcement and first implementation of lock-downs. For the "Vaccine" topic, important press releases and vaccine approvals are linked to structural breaks in the topic. For the "Tier System" topic, each major tier level change was detected as a separate event.

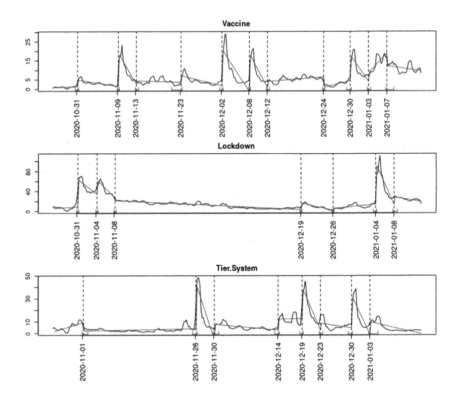

Fig. 7. Event detection for event related topics with Bai-Perron models.

4.4 Detecting Sentiment Changes in User Discussions

To track and identify major change-points in the sentiment of Covid-related discussions, the Bai-Perron model is applied to each topic's sentiment timeline, which represents the fraction of negative tweets per day. Through the integration of topic modelling, sentiment analysis and structural break detection, the framework is now able to not only detect whenever a major shift in the public opinion took place, but also can separate the shifts across different topics. This is useful for the socioeconomic analysis since it can provide a more detailed quantification of the reception of various events within the Twitter active population.

An example can be seen in Fig. 8 where the fraction of negative tweets is displayed for different topics. It can be observed that an event around the 8th to 10th of November lead to an increase in negative tweets for the discussions about politics and 'covidiots', but the sentiment in the restriction discussion remain unchanged. On the other hand, between the 9th and 20th of December, the sentiments for all these topics moved more synchronously, therefore the related events impacted those topics in a similar manner.

Topics	Detected breakpoints	Related real-world events	
"Vaccine"	2020-10-31	2020-10-31	Press conference, Johnson expects vaccine in first quarter of 2021
	2020-11-09 - 2020-11-13	2020-11-09	Pfizer and BioNTech published press release that stated a 90% effectiveness of their candidate
	2020-11-23	2020-11-23	AstraZeneca publishes a press release that stated a 70% efficacy of their candidate
	2020-12-02 - 2020-12-08	2020-12-02	First vaccine against COVID-19 was approved by the Medicines and Healthcare products Regulatory Agency (MHRA) in the United Kingdom
	2020-12-08 - 2020-12-12	2020-12-08	First patient receives a shot of the BioNTech vaccine
	2020-12-24		Christmas
	2020-12-30 - 2021-01-03	2020-12-30	MHRA approves the AstraZeneca vaccine candidate
	2021-12-03 - 2021-01-07	2021-01-04	First patient receives a shot of AstraZeneca's vaccine
	2021-01-07 - END		Wider rollout of the vaccine program
"Lockdown"	2020-12-31 - 2020-11-04	2020-10-31	Boris Johnson announces the second national lockdown
	2020-11-04 - 2020-11-08	2020-11-04	Second national lockdown takes place
	2020-11-08 - 2020-12-19		Long tail of lockdown discussion
	2020-12-19 - 2020-12-26	2020-12-19	Johnson announces that tight restrictions also hold during Christmas
	2021-01-04 - 2021-01-08	2021-01-04	The third lockdown for England and Scotland is announced
"Tier system"	2020-11-01	Late Oct 2020	Various areas reach another tier level within the old 3-level system
	2020-11-26 - 2020-11-30	2020-11-26	Introduction of the new 4-level tier system
	2020-12-14 - 2020-12-19	2020-12-14	London, south and west Essex, and south Hertfordshire are announced to enter Tier 3
	2020-12-19 - 2020-12-23	2020-12-19	Johnson announces that major parts of areas England will enter tier 4
	2020-12-30 - END	2020-12-30	Press conference announces that various other areas are entering tier 4 as well

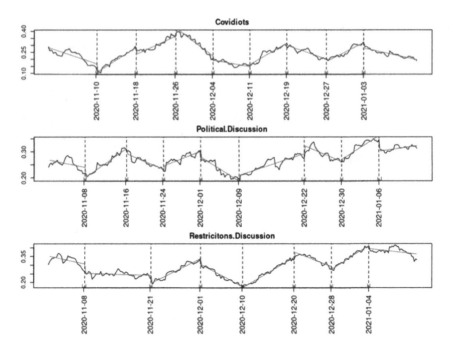

Fig. 8. Detection of sentiment break-point in the daily fraction of negative tweets per topic. An increasing slope reflects an increasing negativity of the sentiment within the topic.

5   Conclusion

Our framework provides an easy to use tool for social scientists to study the discourse on Twitter over time. In particular, it allows the user to detect statistically significant shifts in the sentiment and occurrence of topics. We find that the non-probabilistic NMF algorithm is more suitable for topic modelling on micro-blog document, since it is able to extract topics directly from the original tweets. In contrast, the probabilistic LDA would require the generation of larger pseudo documents via tweet pooling. Furthermore, the properties of NMF in respect to shortness and sparseness are better reflecting the mono-thematic structure of the data.

In a case study about COVID-19 in the UK, we are able extract COVID-19 related topics and their sentiment to gain insights into the discourse during the pandemic. Further, we showed, that with Bai-Perron models the outcomes of the topic models can be used to detect significant shifts in the topic occurrence, that can be matched very well with historical events. In combination with sentiment analysis the same model can help to detect and quantify significant structural breaks in the sentiments per topic.

References

1. Adedoyin-Olowe, M., Gaber, M.M., Dancausa, C.M., Stahl, F., Gomes, J.B.: A rule dynamics approach to event detection in twitter with its application to sports and politics. Expert Syst. Appl. **55**, 351–360 (2016)
2. Andry, A., Wirawan, R., Adhi, N.D.D., Farhan, R., Siti, S.: Dynamic large scale data on twitter using sentiment analysis and topic modeling. In: 2018 6th International Conference on Information and Communication Technology (ICoICT), pp. 254–258 (2018). https://doi.org/10.1109/ICoICT.2018.8528776
3. Antonakaki, D., Fragopoulou, P., Ioannidis, S.: A survey of twitter research: data model, graph structure, sentiment analysis and attacks. Expert Syst. Appl. **164**, 114006 (2021)
4. Bahja, M., Lycett, M.: Identifying patient experience from online resources via sentiment analysis and topic modelling. In: Proceedings of the 3rd IEEE/ACM International Conference on Big Data Computing, Applications and Technologies, BDCAT 2016, New York, NY, USA, pp. 94–99. Association for Computing Machinery (2016). https://doi.org/10.1145/3006299.3006335
5. Bai, J., Perron, P.: Estimating and testing linear models with multiple structural changes. Econometrica **66**(1), 47–78 (1998)
6. Bai, J., Perron, P.: Computation and analysis of multiple structural change models. J. Appl. Economet. **18**(1), 1–22 (2003). https://doi.org/10.1002/jae.659
7. Blei, D.M., Ng, A.Y., Jordan, M.I.: Latent Dirichlet allocation. J. Mach. Learn. Res. **3**(null), 993–1022 (2003)
8. Boutsidis, C., Gallopoulos, E.: SVD based initialization: a head start for nonnegative matrix factorization. Pattern Recogn. **41**(4), 1350–1362 (2008)
9. Févotte, C., Idier, J.: Algorithms for nonnegative matrix factorization with the beta-divergence. CoRR abs/1010.1763 (2010)
10. Ding, C., He, X., Simon, H.D.: On the equivalence of nonnegative matrix factorization and spectral clustering. In: Proceedings of the 2005 SIAM International Conference on Data Mining (SDM), pp. 606–610. https://doi.org/10.1137/1.9781611972757.70
11. Giachanou, A., Crestani, F.: Like it or not: a survey of twitter sentiment analysis methods. ACM Comput. Surv. **49**(2) (2016). https://doi.org/10.1145/2938640
12. Hutto, C., Gilbert, E.: VADER: a parsimonious rule-based model for sentiment analysis of social media text. In: Proceedings of the International AAAI Conference on Web and Social Media, vol. 8, no. 1 (2014). https://ojs.aaai.org/index.php/ICWSM/article/view/14550
13. Johnson, K., Jin, D., Goldwasser, D.: Modeling of political discourse framing on twitter. In: Proceedings of the International AAAI Conference on Web and Social Media, vol. 11, no. 1, May 2017. https://ojs.aaai.org/index.php/ICWSM/article/view/14958
14. Keller, F.B., Schoch, D., Stier, S., Yang, J.: Political astroturfing on twitter: how to coordinate a disinformation campaign. Polit. Commun. **37**(2), 256–280 (2020)
15. Lu, H., Fu, Z., Shu, X.: Non-negative and sparse spectral clustering. Pattern Recogn. **47**(1), 418–426 (2014)

16. Mehrotra, R., Sanner, S., Buntine, W., Xie, L.: Improving LDA topic models for microblogs via tweet pooling and automatic labeling. In: Jones, G.J., Sheridan, P., Kelly, D., de Rijke, M., Sakai, T. (eds.) Proceedings of the 36th International ACM SIGIR Conference on Research and Development in Information Retrieval, New York, NY, USA, pp. 889–892. ACM (2013). https://doi.org/10.1145/2484028.2484166

17. Mohammad, S.M., Bravo-Marquez, F., Salameh, M., Kiritchenko, S.: SemEval-2018 task 1: affect in tweets. In: Proceedings of International Workshop on Semantic Evaluation (SemEval-2018), New Orleans, LA, USA (2018)

18. Patil, P.P., Phansalkar, S., Kryssanov, V.V.: Topic modelling for aspect-level sentiment analysis. In: Kulkarni, A.J., Satapathy, S.C., Kang, T., Kashan, A.H. (eds.) Proceedings of the 2nd International Conference on Data Engineering and Communication Technology. AISC, vol. 828, pp. 221–229. Springer, Singapore (2019). https://doi.org/10.1007/978-981-13-1610-4_23

19. Pedregosa, F., et al.: Scikit-learn: machine learning in Python. J. Mach. Learn. Res. **12**, 2825–2830 (2011)

20. Rill, S., Reinel, D., Scheidt, J., Zicari, R.V.: PoliTwi: early detection of emerging political topics on twitter and the impact on concept-level sentiment analysis. Knowl.-Based Syst. **69**, 24–33 (2014)

21. Roesslein, J.: Tweepy: Twitter for Python! (2020). https://github.com/tweepy/tweepy

22. Severyn, A., Moschitti, A.: Twitter sentiment analysis with deep convolutional neural networks. In: Proceedings of the 38th International ACM SIGIR Conference on Research and Development in Information Retrieval, SIGIR 2015, New York, NY, USA, pp. 959–962. Association for Computing Machinery (2015). https://doi.org/10.1145/2766462.2767830

23. Siegrist, M., Luchsinger, L., Bearth, A.: The impact of trust and risk perception on the acceptance of measures to reduce COVID-19 cases. Risk Anal. (2021). https://doi.org/10.1111/risa.13675

24. Siegrist, M., Zingg, A.: The role of public trust during pandemics. Eur. Psychol. **19**(1), 23–32 (2014). https://doi.org/10.1027/1016-9040/a000169

25. Soares, F.B., Recuero, R., Zago, G.: Influencers in polarized political networks on twitter. In: Proceedings of the 9th International Conference on Social Media and Society, SMSociety 2018, New York, NY, USA, pp. 168–177. Association for Computing Machinery (2018). https://doi.org/10.1145/3217804.3217909

26. Suri, P., Roy, N.R.: Comparison between LDA & NMF for event-detection from large text stream data. In: 2017 3rd International Conference on Computational Intelligence and Communication Technology (CICT), pp. 1–5. IEEE (09022017-10022017). https://doi.org/10.1109/CIACT.2017.7977281

27. Yaqub, U., Chun, S.A., Atluri, V., Vaidya, J.: Analysis of political discourse on twitter in the context of the 2016 US presidential elections. Gov. Inf. Q. **34**(4), 613–626 (2017)

28. Yin, J., Wang, J.: A Dirichlet multinomial mixture model-based approach for short text clustering. In Proceedings of the 20th ACM SIGKDD International Conference on Knowledge Discovery and Data Mining, pp. 233–242 (2014)

29. Chen, Y., Zhang, H., Liu, R., Ye, Z., Lin, J.: Experimental explorations on short text topic mining between LDA and NMF based schemes. Knowl.-Based Syst. **163**, 1–13 (2019)

30. Zeileis, A., Kleiber, C., Krämer, W., Hornik, K.: Testing and dating of structural changes in practice. Comput. Stat. Data Anal. **44**, 109–123 (2003)

31. Zeileis, A., Leisch, F., Hornik, K., Kleiber, C.: strucchange: an R package for testing for structural change in linear regression models. J. Stat. Softw. **7**(2), 1–38 (2002). http://www.jstatsoft.org/v07/i02/
32. Zhou, X., Chen, L.: Event detection over twitter social media streams. VLDB J. **23**(3), 381–400 (2013). https://doi.org/10.1007/s00778-013-0320-3
33. Zimbra, D., Abbasi, A., Zeng, D., Chen, H.: The state-of-the-art in twitter sentiment analysis: a review and benchmark evaluation. ACM Trans. Manage. Inf. Syst. **9**(2) (2018). https://doi.org/10.1145/3185045

Is YouTube Still a Radicalizer? An Exploratory Study on Autoplay and Recommendation

Simon Markmann and Christian Grimme[✉][ID]

Department of Information Systems, University of Münster, Leonardo-Campus 3,
48149 Münster, Germany
{s_mark11,christian.grimme}@uni-muenster.de

Abstract. This work investigates the functioning of YouTube's recommendation system with focus on the autoplay function. The autoplay function was often referred to as "radicalizer" in the past, as it was considered to lead towards more extremist content. By an automated data collection through browser remote control, we simulate different usage scenarios (allowing and disallowing autoplay) with personalized accounts as well as with anonymous users. This leads to multiple recommendation paths, which are analyzed. The presented analyses suggest that while YouTube continues to rely on familiar mechanisms for capturing users' attention, ongoing public criticism with respect to the recommendation system has seemingly led to changes in YouTube's algorithm parameterization and to more cautious recommendations.

Keywords: YouTube · Recommender system · Autoplay · Radicalization · Misinformation

1 Introduction

Recommender systems [2,7] are part of our daily use of the Internet. They are embedded in search engines, in social media, and in trading platforms. As such, they are used - usually unnoticed - by billions of users. These systems go beyond simply 'sorting' unorganized information on the Internet. Unlike early search engines from the ancient days of the Internet, they deliver individualized information (i.e., information tailored to the user or a user group). They try to deduce which information artifacts are useful and which are less helpful with respect to user preferences, semantic contexts, and behavioral patterns [1]. Their superiority in providing mostly appropriate content has largely contributed to the success and market dominance of Google as *the* search engine of our time. In fact, recommender systems are absolutely necessary components of today's platforms and often essential for them to survive in the battle for the attention of Internet users on a relevant scale.

In addition to the (attention) economic benefits of recommendation systems for platforms and users, the social problems associated with these systems are

© Springer Nature Switzerland AG 2021
J. Bright et al. (Eds.): MISDOOM 2021, LNCS 12887, pp. 50–65, 2021.
https://doi.org/10.1007/978-3-030-87031-7_4

increasingly being discussed and highlighted as e.g. by Stöcker [27]. These problems include the use of user interaction as a relevance signal and the misinterpretation of those signals by the recommender system. At the same time, these signals can be deliberately set from the outside to influence the recommendations of the system. The interaction of the user signals, the deliberately designed user interface, the preparation of information and, of course, commercial interests lead to a complex amalgamation that can result in misdevelopments or even radicalization. In a system that classifies user interests on the basis of user signals, captures emotions and combines them with seemingly suitable suggestions to direct attention, there can be no question of informational objectivity and freedom from bias.

YouTube, one of the world's largest video platforms, uses a recommendation system for suggesting videos [10], as do other social media platforms for suggesting other content. The stated goal of this system is, on the one hand, to offer videos to users, which match their interests or satisfy their personal need for information. On the other hand, out of economic interest, users should naturally spend as much time as possible watching videos on the (ad-supported!) platform [20]. At the beginning of 2018, YouTube's Chief Product Officer Neal Mohan stated that 70% of total video consumption (in terms of video viewing time) is due to suggestions from the recommendation system [26]. In addition to the actual video being viewed, YouTube displays other recommended videos. In 2015, YouTube also introduced an autoplay function, which automatically recommends another video at the end of a watched video and plays it automatically without user interaction [5].

However, the recommendation system of YouTube, which most of the time works inconspicuously for users, sometimes attract attention by making and realizing (in the autoplay case) recommendations that seem unusual or even frightening and dangerous. For example, in the context of the 2016 U.S. election campaign, the New York Times reported YouTube as "The great radicalizer" [31] and noted that extreme videos on YouTube quickly became part of the recommendations. The autoplay function in particular is attributed with the property of delivering radical or inappropriate content, disinformation and fake news [19,24], and in some cases even promoting a convergence toward this content [28,31] (also in the sense of a filter bubble [22]).

Also as a reaction to these reports and their public resonance, YouTube has recently announced in many blogs and articles [14,21,32] that it will react to problematic algorithmic behavior and adapt its recommender system. This should be accompanied not least by measures that promote quality content and combat fake news and disinformation.

Since YouTube's business model is of course centrally based on its recommendation system, the algorithms and possible changes are classified as a trade secret and are not disclosed. An audit of the announced measures is only carried out by YouTube itself and is difficult to perform in an independent way. From a methodological point of view, external testing of these announcements means, above all, that the functioning of the recommender system (as a black box) must continue to be challenged on a regular basis.

This work reports a recent experimental and exploratory study focusing in particular on the autoplay mechanism and its functioning. Therefore, the study follows the autoplay recommendations for several steps "in depth" and analyzes the diversity or convergence of recommendation paths - starting from different profiles and subject areas. This is a first systematic, experimental step towards evaluating previous models, simulations, and observations as e.g. reported by Stöcker and Preuss [28].

In addition, however, other current features of the recommender system can be derived from the experimentally collected data, allowing limited insight into the recommender's operation and thus some speculation on the design and control issues that arise for YouTube with the recommender system and its public perception.

After a brief review of the literature in the context of this work in Sect. 2, the next Sect. 3 moves on to the experimental design. Section 4 presents and analyses the results. Eventually, Sect. 5 discusses the results, the necessity to further investigate recommender systems in platforms, and points to an inherent design and control problem for YouTube.

2   Related Work

Scientific analysis of commercial recommender systems faces the major problem that these systems are considered trade secrets of the companies which use them [23]. This secrecy of algorithms and processed data is essential for the economic existence of the companies whose entire business model is based on these recommender systems. In this respect, an investigation of these black box systems from the outside is always limited and only of restricted significance. At the same time, however, it is important that these investigations - be they individual observations or systematic surveys of specific aspects - are carried out. They allow small insights into complex systems such as search engines or even video platforms such as YouTube, but in their totality they can also provide a framework for simulating [28] and even evaluating these systems, including in terms of individual or societal impact [11,33].

We briefly consider here some of these approaches to what is often called auditing of recommender systems. We specifically focus on the context of YouTube, the impact of these audits on public perception, and the response of the platform itself.

2.1   Analyzing How the YouTube Recommender Might Work

As mentioned before, YouTube's recommendation system is a black box and can only be analyzed to a limited extent by external parties. An analysis always means that aspects of the system can be checked for their behavior in a very selective way. Already very early investigations, which often focused on measuring popularity development of videos in YouTube's platform [8], relied on crawling data from the platform [8,35] or on additional measurement of network activity, e.g. at an university campus [37]. Other approaches used search queries and crawling as strategies to acquire insights into personalization [13] of content delivery by YouTube. Only very rare publications of YouTube itself allow some restricted insights into the recommender system. As such YouTube published in 2012 that it had reconfigured video recommendation to weight watch time more strongly [20]. In 2016, some developers of the recommender AI presented the basic structure of the filtering and recommendation system (using deep learning) without providing too much detail [10]. Most interesting, the recommender system is - according to the developers - parameterizable. This ensures that the YouTube product can be adjusted constantly regarding its behavior. This large dynamic of the recommender system makes a reliable analysis and an explanation of observed effects even more difficult. Therefore, on the one hand, it is important to continuously re-survey the behavior of the recommendation system [15,16]. On the other hand, approaches like those of Stöcker and Preuss [28] are worth emphasizing. Based on insights gained so far through other studies and YouTube's publications, the authors have created a simple simulation model to study the effects of autoplay and demonstrate observed effects (such as the convergence of autoplay recommendations towards problematic content).

This paper fits into the context of the ongoing investigation of YouTube's recommendation system, and at the same time tries to pick up some of the previous findings and simulation results in order to assess YouTube's development - also under the impression of the larger public perception of societal issues with recommendations.

2.2 Issues with Recommendations in YouTube

In recent years, scientific research, various experiments and newspaper reports or data journalistic investigations have had an ever-increasing impact on the perception of YouTube's recommendation system, which actually works in the background. Former employees of YouTube and journalists have analyzed the proposals of the YouTube recommender system - especially in the context of the US presidential election in 2016 - and found that this system was able to help extreme and radical content gain visibility [17,18,31]. In a paper on the major social media platforms as an ecosystem for disinformation, Stöcker [27] reports on various examples that show that the optimization of criteria such as watch time can lead to the disproportionate presentation of radical or conspiracy-theory content, as can a focus on the frequency of clicks on a video or ratings. In the context of science communication, Allgaier [3] confirms this assessment and provides another example: he experimentally demonstrates that the recommendation system disproportionately suggests video content, which contradicts the mainstream science in the context of climate change.

These insights and their media reappraisal have certainly contributed significantly to the critical view of the public on YouTube's recommendation system (and also the systems of other platforms). In the context of YouTube, this can also be seen in two very recent surveys: in their study Zimmermann et al. [36] report on young people's consumption of YouTube content on political and social issues and find greater skepticism about the trustworthiness of the content presented there. The videos on the YouTube platform are seen as more entertaining than classically produced TV content. At the same time, however, YouTube content is also described as less objective, opinion-oriented, more emotional, and less credible. Further it is considered to be manipulative. Another study reveals that people live in an ambivalent relationship with recommendation systems [4]: On the one hand, people rarely trust the decisions of artificial decision makers. At the same time, a majority of respondents are convinced that artificially intelligent recommendation systems make better decisions than human decision-makers do.

The scientific study of YouTube's recommendation system and the media discussion partly based on it thus seem to influence also the perception of recommendation systems among users of YouTube and other platforms. It can be assumed that these reactions have contributed to the fact that, on the one hand, regulatory considerations have been made and, at the same time, containment measures have been announced by YouTube [14, 21, 32].

Interestingly, a recent dissertation [15] research (and conducted parallel to this study) investigates the recommender system by following suggestions in an automated way and concludes that some of the previously observed and reported anomalies (especially the convergence to critical content) are no longer present. The study could be seen as a first indication of changes in YouTube's recommendation system. However, the data basis is still very insufficient even for a preliminary statement - also due to a limited number of experiments conducted in the mentioned study. This study strives for providing further exploratory experiments and thus additional insights into the functioning of the recommendation system in order to build a first picture of YouTube's reactions and their effects.

3   Experimental Design

The recommendation system of YouTube is examined with the help of an exploratory experiment. The focus is on the video suggestions that are displayed on the right side of the website when a video is played. This investigation is intended to provide insights into the underlying algorithmic systematic of the platform. Although this work focuses on data collection along the automated recommendations of the autoplay function, additional information is collected during this process. This allows additional analysis and inductive research based on the gathered data.

Figure 1 shows the general setting of the implemented experiment. YouTube-offered videos from different categories were played with 30 personalized accounts. After finishing a video, the next suggested autoplay video was allowed to start, finally resulting in a graph of videos with start and end nodes at a

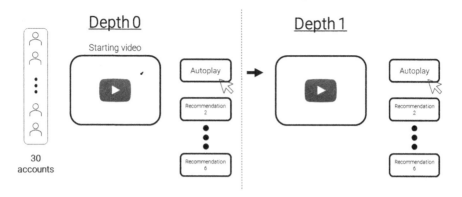

Fig. 1. The created accounts start the experiment by watching a prior chosen video in 'depth 0' and play the first recommended video afterwards, which is the video of the autoplay function. This process is executed for each run until 'depth 10'.

depth of 10. The watched videos were saved along with the top-five video recommendations at each stage. All relevant information about the collected videos, the users, and the runs were stored in a database to be analyzed afterwards.

This setting provided a database of almost 30,000 video recommendations collected between February and March 2021 to expose underlying mechanisms of YouTube's recommender system. These videos were automatically played on a server of the University of Münster, partly with logged-in accounts and partly without accounts. As the server was operated behind a shared IP address, watch histories cannot be allocated directly to one person by YouTube. At the same time, however, this limits the variety of possible users to people who have access to this network, to academics and students, making it not representative for the German population.

Out of these 30 accounts 28 were manually created while two had already been actively used before. The accounts were created with the intention to appear as realistic as possible and also to represent a sample size of randomly chosen YouTube users. To achieve this, first personal profiles were created for each account, which took into consideration demographic aspects like age or gender as well as personal interests. The average age of the users was 35 with more young users than older ones and the genders were evenly distributed. These aspects were aligned to a statistic of YouTube user demographics [29].

Subsequently each of the accounts watched ten to fifteen videos in a clean browser to give the recommender system a chance for classifying them according to their account properties and interests. 'Clean' means that the browser data got deleted every time an account watched a couple of videos and the users changed web browsers in order to hinder YouTube in spotting links between accounts. Each account played videos that were partly random and partly inspired by their demographic aspects. Here the goal was to get many distinct video topics but also some overlapping ones. In the end each user had his or her own distinct starting page with video recommendations of which the first 20 videos also got collected.

The users (or no user) played each video for a relative amount of time. This amount was either 5%, 50% or 95% of the videos duration. After the completion of each run, the search history got deleted which led to no traces of activity in the recommendations of the starting pages.

To determine whether the recommender system behaves different for individual video categories, four starting videos were chosen. The first video (News) was selected as a daily news video from the German channel ZDF, which is a public broadcaster. The next video (Music) was a music video of a song by the American artist Post Malone. The third video (Covid) dealt with the Covid-19 crisis. The video cannot be found directly via the search bar anymore and it criticizes a famous German virologist and the WHO. The last video (Trend) was a short video from the trend section that got re-uploaded from the platform TikTok. It shows a family doing a funny challenge. Time and capacity limits lead to the conclusion that four starting videos would be the maximum. The categories 'News' and 'Covid' are of social and political interest and center of critique which is why they were chosen, also because 'News' is a big section on YouTube. 'Music' is the category with YouTube's most watched videos. 'Trend' is full of videos that are currently famous and full of different types of created content.

For the automated data collection, a script was created, which initiated a Google Chrome web driver with the help of the test-software Selenium. This driver can start either with or without the user data of the accounts. This also allows video suggestions to be collected that are not dependent on the users' profiles. The script can then be executed for different starting videos, numbers of runs and percentages of watch time and it collects the URL addresses of the autoplay videos and five other recommended videos. The autoplay video is the video, which is recommended first for each watched video and starts automatically after a video ends, if the autoplay function is not deactivated. For the automated skipping of advertisements, an additional browser extension was downloaded from the Chrome Web Store, customized with the help of another script, and added to the web driver. The video URLs were then fed into the YouTube Data API and the outputs were saved with the user data into a SQL-based database.

4 Experiments

The following chapter provides insights into the collected data. Mainly, the diversity of the recommendations was compared to each other, the starting page, the relative playing time, the autoplay function or to the non-personalised suggestions. Furthermore, metadata such as video length, ratings or number of views were examined.

What Are the Effects on the Length of the Videos?
In the following, the influence of the various parameters on the duration of the suggested videos is analyzed. For this part of the evaluation, all videos longer than two hours were omitted, as it is unrealistic that overlong videos will be watched in their entirety. These long videos are often summarized live-streams or music compilations. In addition, these outliers strongly distort the statistics of the data.

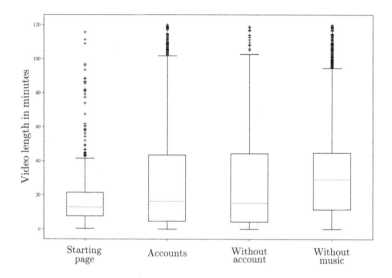

Fig. 2. The video lengths of the proposals seem to be generally longer than the videos of the starting pages. Especially without the category 'Music' there is a sharp difference.

Figure 2 shows box plots of the lengths of the videos of the users' starting pages, the recommended videos of the users, in comparison those without logged-in users and the recommendations without the category 'Music'.

We will exclude the category 'Music' oftentimes during the following evaluations, since the system acts significantly different for this category. About 73% of the channels that appear in this category have the channel tag 'Music' and most of the videos are between three and five minutes long. This segmentation makes sense for both YouTube and the user, since YouTube is used as a music platform by a lot of users and music videos have the most views [30].

It is apparent from Fig. 2 that the suggested videos are longer compared to those on the starting page, especially without the category 'Music'. Note that the videos of the starting pages (without the omitted overlong videos) are 18:30 min long at median *and* the starting videos of the three categories are also each shorter than 16 min. There is no significant difference between the personalized and non-personalised suggestions.

Additionally the video lengths of the runs in which videos were played for a short, medium, or long amount of time are compared. The category 'Music' is again omitted because the data of this category scatters minimally around three to five minutes and thus weakens the effects for the other categories. The difference in the mean values of the long and short watched videos is 9:59 min. The Wilcoxon rank sum test for the median video lengths of the runs as random variables yields a p-value of 4.5277×10^{-117}. The hypothesis that the median lengths of the long and short watched video runs is the same, can therefore be rejected.

How Diverse Are the Recommendations for Different Users?
Table 1 shows for each depth of the runs how many of the recommended videos were suggested to more than one of the 30 users. The measured values were further subdivided into the four categories and the relative amount of video watching. The values range from 0 to 100%, where 100 (%) states that every video recommendation appeared in all of the thirty users. A value of 0 (%) on the other hand indicates that no video recommendation appeared more than once. Intermediate values should be interpreted accordingly. If there is an effect that groups the 30 users and could thus indicate filter bubbles or similar undesirable effects, then the percentage values should at least not flatten out completely. However, as can be seen, especially in the 'trend' category, the common video suggestions seem to disappear completely.

Table 1. Proportion (in %) of **videos** occurring multiple times per depth of a run across the 30 subjects.

Depth of run	News		Music		Trend		Covid-19	
	Short	Long	Short	Long	Short	Long	Short	Long
1	43	47	75	74	24	26	22	36
2	14	22	53	67	23	21	16	19
3	13	14	38	58	16	18	12	18
4	13	11	33	51	9	12	9	17
5	10	14	21	44	6	10	13	12
6	14	15	10	43	3	4	11	13
7	7	12	9	40	6	1	9	11
8	7	14	7	37	3	2	6	12
9	8	13	10	31	1	0	6	11
10	7	11	7	26	2	1	1	11

The partly high percentages for the music videos can again be explained by the fact that YouTube seems to be transforming into a music platform for these videos. In this case, similar songs are played rather than suggesting user-specific videos. For news videos, there seem to be cases of groupings. These connections rarely involve more than two users and are rather caused by the fact that there is only a limited amount of channels that get recommended in this category. In general, for news videos, it is almost mainly documentaries or news from other news channels that are suggested. As long as videos are watched for a long time, videos from a similar category continue to be suggested. In the category 'Covid-19', too, mainly documentaries or talk shows were suggested, which rarely contained inappropriate or false content. The only user for whom there were partially critical recommendations, as evidenced by the fact that the suggestions were politically one-sided, is the one who also played exclusively one-sided political content in the course of the personalization. A comparison of the channels that uploaded the video recommendations in the two similar-looking categories returns a rather high value of 0.652 for the cosine similarity[1]. In comparison, the categories 'News' and 'Trend' have a cosine similarity of 0.043.

Table 2. Proportion (in %) of **channels** occurring multiple times per depth of a run across the 30 subjects.

Depth of run	News		Music		Trend		Covid-19	
	Short	Long	Short	Long	Short	Long	Short	Long
1	74	79	73	69	25	32	49	54
2	62	62	57	69	21	23	42	46
3	50	53	46	63	19	18	46	54
4	45	54	46	56	20	16	40	47
5	40	51	31	51	13	13	35	38
6	44	49	20	53	13	10	34	39
7	43	51	20	52	11	3	33	40
8	35	48	15	56	6	6	27	32
9	31	54	20	53	5	0	27	30
10	31	52	14	45	5	3	17	35

The same methodology was used for the channels that uploaded these videos. Table 2 shows how many of the channels were recommended more than once per depth. Again a value of 100 (%) would indicate that the same channels got recommended for all of the 30 accounts per depth of the run and a value of 0 (%) would show no same channel recommendations. It was expected that the values would be at least as high as those of the videos. In a few places this is not the case, as some videos were deleted by the platform before they were inserted into the API and therefore do not appear for the channels, but for

---

[1] The cosine similarity [25] is computed as angle between two vectors, which represent the frequency distribution of video tags in the compared categories. A value of 0 denotes maximum dissimilarity, while a value of 1 denotes equality.

the videos. Once again, there is a slightly recognizable difference between the different relative duration of the played videos.

Does It Matter How Long Videos are Watched?
Another investigation was conducted on the consumption duration of watched videos, which collected the average number of unique channels per total run. This metric is meaningful because a low number of unique channels cannot in any way indicate high diversity. The long and short watched videos respectively provide a mean of 20.02 and 28.97 unique channels per run. This means that the 60 videos collected in one run originate on average from 20 different channels in the first case and from 29 different channels in the second case. The Wilcoxon test returns a p-value of 8.5433×10^{-20} for the two distributions. The hypothesis that long or short viewing has no influence on the number of unique channels per run can be rejected at any relevant level of significance. The recommendation system notices when a user skips videos, considers this as negative feedback, and tries (as a kind of compensation strategy) to vary the content, or at least the channels for matching the users interests (again).

Does the Autoplay Function Act Different?
The autoplay function was analyzed by comparing the channel that uploaded the next video with the previous one. If video A from channel C starts and video B from channel C is suggested next, we assume that the suggestions do not differ strongly. For the autoplay videos, this happens 57.17% of the time for the 30 accounts. Even without users, this value is in a similar range at 58.75%. For the remaining five video suggestions of each run, the values are 29.62% and 32.23% respectively. The Wilcoxon rank sum test gives a p-value of 4.2642×10^{-45} for accounts and 1.6373×10^{-16} without an account. The random variables in this test are the values of the average consecutive same channels in the runs. This shows that the autoplay function tends to suggest more videos of the same channel. Breaking this further down into categories shows that this effect is slightly stronger for news videos (61.11%) and weaker for music videos (50%). There is also a difference for the breakdown between long and short viewing: 64.5% of the channels match their previous one for long viewing, whereas it is only 49.58% for short viewing. Testing the hypothesis that short and long viewing have an equal median for this random variable can be rejected with a p-value of 7.4756×10^{-9}. The measured values of the autoplay condition are generally high and accordingly also had an influence on the other results, since in each case the autoplay video was played next. If one of the other five videos had been played instead, the collected data and the resulting analysis could have deviated strongly.

How Does the System Change for a Personalized Account?
The difference between video recommendations with or without an account in terms of content diversity has not been considered, yet. Once again, the average number of unique channels per run was calculated. This is $\mu = 24.08$ with a standard deviation of $\sigma = 8.97$ for accounts and $\mu = 23.11$ with $\sigma = 8.09$ for

no account. Under these circumstances, the use of an account does not seem to have a great influence on the calculated parameter. A comparison of the collected channels of the video suggestions with or without an account results in a value of 0.748 for the cosine similarity. This high value can be justified with the already mentioned characteristics of the categories 'Music', 'Covid-19' and 'News'. Moreover, the runs started on the same videos.

Ratings, Clicks and Content Partnerships
The ratio of likes to dislikes for the video suggestions is 4:1, that is, 79% of the ratings are positive. Note that only 1.86% of the videos were rated. For 85% of the video suggestions there are even more than 90% positive ratings and only 0.5% of the suggestions have more negative than positive ratings. The latter are mainly videos about Germany's Covid-19 policy.

The average number of views is 138,718,992. This value breaks down for the four categories as follows: 'Music': 527,544,424, 'News': 1,424,238, 'Covid-19': 2,085,894 and 'Trend': 23,389,197. For each of the categories, the value is increased compared to the initially chosen video. The videos of the users' home pages were viewed on average 20,119,423. Moreover, the platform seems to favor the biggest channels when it comes to the order of suggestions and directs the user to videos from these channels via autoplay. For example, for the category 'Trend', the three channels that account for the most suggestions in depth 10 have an average subscriber base of 32 million, placing them among the largest channels on YouTube; 75.32% of the suggested videos are from channels that have a partnership with YouTube that allows them to monetize their videos.

5 Discussion and Conclusion

The results of this study show that YouTube has retained features of the recommendation system in many areas despite criticism from outside. As already confirmed in previous studies and also by YouTube itself, the recommendation system tends to suggest longer videos starting from the initial video. At the same time, the consumption duration of videos is used as a rating or satisfaction measure as feedback to the system. This is also important because the percentage of direct user ratings per video view is only about 1.86%. Thus, individual rating responses by users would not be sufficient as feedback for the recommender.

At the same time, however, the study showed that playing videos with and without an account has neither a significant influence on the diversity of the suggestions nor on the length of the videos. However, due to the fact that the recommendation system includes the watching history of an account, the suggestions for users with logged in account fit well with the previously set interests. It can be speculated that the basic functionality of suggestion generation is the same, but history is an important influencing factor - also in order to fit content to user preferences and to preserve their attention and interest in watching further content.

When looking at the autoplay function, we were able to show that this leads to a lower diversity of suggestions. However, the restriction of diversity refers to the channels, not videos. Again, the selection is influenced by the overall account watching history, but the immediate history also seems to be weighted more heavily.

It is also noticeable that the developers of the recommendation algorithm apparently provide quite different parameterizations for different categories. While YouTube apparently 'mutates' into a music platform for the music category, news channels and channels critical of governmental Covid-19 measures, for example, are treated very similarly when it comes to suggesting content. Especially in the last category, mainstream content (news, talk shows, and documentaries) is suggested to compensate for criticism presented. This can be interpreted as a manifestation of YouTube's responses to persistent criticism of the recommendation system.

The present results (cautiously) suggest that YouTube's interventions in the recommendation system show some effects. By its own admission, YouTube is very active in combating problematic content[2]. Its latest transparency report shows that YouTube has already removed more than 2 million channels and close to 10 million videos in the first three months of 2021[3]. Both YouTube's response and consideration of the characteristics of the recommendation system allow for two conclusions:

1. The continuous external analysis and monitoring of the Black Box recommendation system, despite their mostly exemplary nature, can be helpful to uncover problems and needs for action and thus influence (also through public discussion) the development of these systems. This can and should motivate scientists and journalists to continue to critically question the decisions of automated systems.
2. The investigation and the apparent adaptation of the decision-making system, while at the same time maintaining various optimization goals of the recommender system, suggest that platforms like YouTube are in a dichotomy between public pressure due to decision errors and the economic necessity of the recommender system (and thus the necessity to accept deviations from 'normal'). If YouTube follows the rules of exploiting users' attention (see also attention economy [6,12,34]), it cannot completely dispense with stimuli that keep users completely away from surprising new content - perhaps even content tending toward the extreme or sensational - in an attention-binding spiral [11]. Therefore, YouTube (unless regulations force it) will certainly continue to offer problematic content. Filtering content only when it enters the system or when moderation is triggered by users are only partly effective measures.

---

[2] https://blog.youtube/news-and-events/more-information-faster-removals-more/.
[3] https://transparencyreport.google.com/youtube-policy/removals?hl=en.

Limitations

Just like any other study of black box systems, the presented experiments have limitations. The collection of recommendations originated from four different starting videos. For other videos the results could be different. Furthermore, the results can only be verified for the time span of February till March of 2021 as afterwards the system could have changed significantly (due to new parameterization by YouTube). Also the sample size is rather small and could be influenced subjectively as the accounts were created manually. The assumption, that users always follow the autoplay function is also possibly unrealistic. Although it was the explicit focus of this study, several (possibly more realistic) configurations of user interaction are still open to be investigated.

Future Work

The data collection methodology presented here (and related methods in previous work, e.g. [15]) provides the ability to automatically and systematically collect data on the behavior of YouTube's recommender system. It is important that analogous experiments are repeated to verify the presented analyses and to track developments in the YouTube system over time. At the same time, however, analyzing the effects and the impact of scientific and media reports on how recommender systems work in an interesting field of research beyond statistical evaluation. The question of how people deal with machine decisions and which social and concrete economic effects these systems have needs to be further investigated from a diverse and interdisciplinary perspective (see e.g. [9] on open aspects in algorithmization, attention economy, and ethics).

Acknowlegments. Both authors appreciate the support of the European Research Center for Information Systems (ERCIS).

References

1. Adomavicius, G., Tuzhilin, A.: Toward the next generation of recommender systems: a survey of the state-of-the-art and possible extensions. IEEE Trans. Knowl. Data Eng. **17**(6), 734–749 (2005). https://doi.org/10.1109/TKDE.2005.99
2. Aggarwal, C.C.: Recommender Systems: The Textbook. Springer, Cham (2016). https://doi.org/10.1007/978-3-319-29659-3
3. Allgaier, J.: Science and environmental communication on YouTube: strategically distorted communications in online videos on climate change and climate engineering. Front. Commun. **4**, 36 (2019). https://doi.org/10.3389/fcomm.2019.00036
4. Araujo, T., Helberger, N., Kruikemeier, S., de Vreese, C.H.: In AI we trust? Perceptions about automated decision-making by artificial intelligence. AI Soc. **35**(3), 611–623 (2020). https://doi.org/10.1007/s00146-019-00931-w
5. Brinkmann, M.: Google tests new video autoplay feature on YouTube (2015). https://www.ghacks.net/2015/01/28/google-tests-new-video-autoplay-feature-on-youtube/. Accessed 29 Mar 2021
6. Brynjolfsson, E., Oh, J.: The attention economy: measuring the value of free digital services on the internet. In: ICIS 2012 Proceedings (2012)

7. Burke, R., Felfernig, A., Göker, M.H.: Recommender systems: an overview. AI Mag. **32**(3), 13–18 (2011). https://doi.org/10.1609/aimag.v32i3.2361

8. Cha, M., Kwak, H., Rodriguez, P., Ahn, Y.Y., Moon, S.: I tube, you tube, everybody tubes: analyzing the world's largest user generated content video system. In: Proceedings of the 7th ACM SIGCOMM Conference on Internet Measurement, IMC 2007, New York, NY, USA, pp. 1–14. Association for Computing Machinery (2007). https://doi.org/10.1145/1298306.1298309

9. Coombs, C., et al.: What is it about humanity that we can't give away to intelligent machines? A European perspective. Int J. Inf. Manag. **58** (2021). https://doi.org/10.1016/j.ijinfomgt.2021.102311

10. Covington, P., Adams, J., Sargin, E.: Deep neural networks for YouTube recommendations. In: Proceedings of the 10th ACM Conference on Recommender Systems, RecSys 2016, New York, NY, USA, pp. 191–198. Association for Computing Machinery (2016). https://doi.org/10.1145/2959100.2959190

11. Eyal, N., Hoover, R.: Hooked - How to Build Habit-Forming Products. Penguin Publishing Group, New York (2014)

12. Goldhaber, M.H.: The attention economy and the Net. First Monday (1997). https://doi.org/10.5210/fm.v2i4.519

13. Hannak, A., et al.: Measuring personalization of web search. In: Proceedings of the 22nd International Conference on World Wide Web, WWW 2013, New York, NY, USA, pp. 527–538. Association for Computing Machinery (2013). https://doi.org/10.1145/2488388.2488435

14. Hern, A.: YouTube to manually review popular videos before placing ads, January 2018. http://www.theguardian.com/technology/2018/jan/17/youtube-google-manually-review-top-videos-before-placing-ads-scandal-logan-paul

15. Heuer, H.: Users & machine learning-based curation systems. Ph.D. thesis, University of Bremen, Bremen, July 2020

16. Hussein, E., Juneja, P., Mitra, T.: Measuring misinformation in video search platforms: an audit study on YouTube. Proc. ACM Hum. Comput. Interact. **4**(CSCW1), 1–27 (2020)

17. Lewis, P.: 'Fiction is outperforming reality': how YouTube's algorithm distorts truth, February 2018. http://www.theguardian.com/technology/2018/feb/02/how-youtubes-algorithm-distorts-truth

18. Lewis, P., McCormick, E.: How an ex-YouTube insider investigated its secret algorithm, February 2018. http://www.theguardian.com/technology/2018/feb/02/youtube-algorithm-election-clinton-trump-guillaume-chaslot

19. Maack, M.: 'YouTube recommendations are toxic', says dev who worked on the algorithm (2019). https://thenextweb.com/google/2019/06/14/youtube-recommendations-toxic-algorithm-google-ai/. Accessed 26 Mar 2021

20. Meyerson, E.: YouTube now: why we focus on watch time (2012). https://blog.youtube/news-and-events/youtube-now-why-we-focus-on-watch-time/

21. Newton, C.: YouTube says it will recommend fewer videos about conspiracy theories, January 2019. https://www.theverge.com/2019/1/25/18197301/youtube-algorithm-conspiracy-theories-misinformation

22. Pariser, E.: The Filter Bubble: What the Internet is Hiding From You. Penguin, London (2011)

23. Pasquale, F.: The Black Box Society. Harvard University Press, Cambridge (2015)

24. Rieder, B., Matamoros-Fernández, A., Coromina, Ò.: From ranking algorithms to 'ranking cultures' investigating the modulation of visibility in YouTube search results. Convergence **24**(1), 50–68 (2018)

25. Singhal, A.: Modern information retrieval: a brief overview. IEEE Data Eng. Bull. **24**(4), 35–43 (2001)

26. Solsman, J.E.: YouTube's AI is the puppet master over most of what you watch (2018). https://www.cnet.com/news/youtube-ces-2018-neal-mohan/. Accessed 8 Mar 2021

27. Stöcker, C.: How facebook and google accidentally created a perfect ecosystem for targeted disinformation. In: Grimme, C., Preuss, M., Takes, F.W., Waldherr, A. (eds.) MISDOOM 2019. LNCS, vol. 12021, pp. 129–149. Springer, Cham (2020). https://doi.org/10.1007/978-3-030-39627-5_11

28. Stöcker, C., Preuss, M.: Riding the wave of misclassification: how we end up with extreme YouTube content. In: Meiselwitz, G. (ed.) HCII 2020. LNCS, vol. 12194, pp. 359–375. Springer, Cham (2020). https://doi.org/10.1007/978-3-030-49570-1_25

29. Tankovska, H.: Most popular social networks worldwide as of January 2021, ranked by number of active users (2021). https://www.statista.com/statistics/272014/global-social-networks-ranked-by-number-of-users/. Accessed 24 Mar 2021

30. Tankovska, H.: Most popular YouTube videos based on total global views as of February 2021 (2021). https://www.statista.com/statistics/249396/top-youtube-videos-views/. Accessed 30 Mar 2021

31. Tufekci, Z.: YouTube, the Great Radicalizer. The New York Times, March 2018. https://www.nytimes.com/2018/03/10/opinion/sunday/youtube-politics-radical.html

32. Waterson, J.: YouTube bans videos promoting Nazi ideology, June 2019. http://www.theguardian.com/technology/2019/jun/05/youtube-bans-videos-promoting-nazi-ideology

33. Williams, J.: Stand Out of Our Light: Freedom and Resistance in the Attention Economy. Cambridge University Press, Cambridge (2018). https://doi.org/10.1017/9781108453004

34. Zhang, Y., Goh, K.H.: Attracting versus sustaining attention in the information economy. In: Cho, W., Fan, M., Shaw, M.J., Yoo, B., Zhang, H. (eds.) WEB 2017. LNBIP, vol. 328, pp. 1–14. Springer, Cham (2018). https://doi.org/10.1007/978-3-319-99936-4_1

35. Zhou, R., Khemmarat, S., Gao, L.: The impact of YouTube recommendation system on video views. In: Proceedings of the 10th ACM SIGCOMM Conference on Internet Measurement, IMC 2010, New York, NY, USA, pp. 404–410. Association for Computing Machinery (2010). https://doi.org/10.1145/1879141.1879193

36. Zimmermann, D., et al.: Influencers on YouTube: a quantitative study on young people's use and perception of videos about political and societal topics. Curr. Psychol. (3), 1–17 (2020). https://doi.org/10.1007/s12144-020-01164-7

37. Zink, M., Suh, K., Gu, Y., Kurose, J.: Characteristics of YouTube network traffic at a campus network - measurements, models, and implications. Comput. Netw. Int. J. Comput. Telecommun. Netw. **53**(4), 501–514 (2009). https://doi.org/10.1016/j.comnet.2008.09.022

Understanding the Impact of and Analysing Fake News About COVID-19 in SA

Sthembile Mthethwa[(⊠)], Nelisiwe Dlamini, Nenekazi Mkuzangwe, Avuya Shibambu, Thato Boateng, and Motlatsi Mantsi

Defense and Security, Council for Scientific and Industrial Research, Pretoria 0001, South Africa
smthethwa@csir.co.za

Abstract. The topic of fake news is not new but its rise is fueled by the digital age era. The increased proliferation of fake news has been observed since the coronavirus disease 2019 (COVID-19) started, thus introducing controversy regarding its origin, conspiracies about 5G causing COVID-19 and COVID-19 home remedies or prevention methods. This information may be harmless, or could potentially pose a threat by misleading the population to depend on unjustified and unsubstantiated claims. Several studies worldwide are investing towards this topic, however, very little has been done in the South African context. Therefore, this study aims at analysing fake news about COVID-19 spread during the South African national lockdown on social media platforms and news outlets; together with the measures put in place by the government i.e. social relief funds and food parcels. This study took place between March 2020 and October 2020 whereby a Google form was used to collect data. The collected data was verified using fact-checking websites like Africa Check and techniques such as Google reverse image for image verification. Thereafter, the data was coded according to these categories, namely; misinformation, disinformation, malinformation, propaganda and scams, and annotated according to 11 annotation classes. The analysis showed that Twitter was the leading source of fake news at 59% followed by WhatsApp at 22%. In addition, most discussions were in reference to COVID-19 cures and treatments. Overtime, a correlation was observed between events (e.g., change in regulations) that occurred and the spread of fake news. To dispel and delegitimise the sources, a publicly accessible dashboard was created where all verified fake news were shared for easier access. This study has established an understanding of the nature of fake news and draws insights that offer practical guidance on how fake news may be combated in the future.

Keywords: COVID-19 · Misinformation · Social media

1 Introduction

Social media has changed drastically in the past few years from being just a means of entertainment to becoming a daily part of our lives [1]. Websites and applications that allow the fast transfer of information in the form of short texts, links, videos or photos [2], have transformed the way we work and communicate immensely. This has resulted

© Springer Nature Switzerland AG 2021
J. Bright et al. (Eds.): MISDOOM 2021, LNCS 12887, pp. 66–84, 2021.
https://doi.org/10.1007/978-3-030-87031-7_5

in it having great influence on all aspects of our lives. Participating on social media discussions is very simple, only the creation of an account is required and afterward, one can create, share and engage in discussions [2]. This has had a rather dramatic impact when it comes to how stories and opinions are shared, giving people access to important stories and latest in-formation. However, with the easy distribution of information, the spread of fake news is one of the downsides of social media. Nowadays, a simple retweet or share diffuses fake news more rapidly than before [3]. Social media has become the most influential source of uncensored information and it has become harder to distinguish between what is true and what is not [4]. Studies show that 62% of United States (US) adults get their news on social media, one of the sources being Facebook [5].

Since the emergence of the coronavirus disease 2019 (COVID-19), the spread of fake news has been very alarming. COVID-19 has posed a concern to the health of many humans globally [6]. When the World Health Organization (WHO) declared the virus as a global pandemic on 11 March 2020, this caused a panic to many. It rapidly spread in a short space of time, "the number of cases outside China increased 13-fold and the number of countries with cases in-creased threefold" [6]. The fact that COVID-19 is an illness with incomplete clinical knowledge on the cause and treatment led to a gap that allowed many to speculate as they had limited facts [7].

The spread of misleading information about COVID-19 has led to the WHO to warn of an-ongoing "infodemic" which is an overabundance of information – especially mis-information – during an epidemic [8]. This makes it harder for people to find trustworthy and reliable information when they need it. Thus, we have experienced a surge of fake news since COVID-19 was reported, it has been at the center of fake news [9] and has made headlines on various social media platforms [10]. The spread of fake news related to COVID-19 covers a range of topics, and some of the common fake news topics range from COVID-19 treatment, home remedies, COVID-19 origin and general human behavior. A lot of people were led to believe that COVID-19 could be cured by drinking salty water and drinking bleach [11]. Other prominent fake news attached to COVID-19 include conspiracy theories about its source whereby the Chinese government was blamed for creating COVID-19 [9] due to the fact that the first case was discovered in China. This just goes to show how fake news has great influence on people's perceptions, beliefs and actions [9].

Fake news is a worldwide problem and countless studies have been conducted to address its impact including finding various methods to detect and dispel fake news [12]. Despite the vast research that is available, it is not prevalent in South Africa (SA) and not much is drawn from the spread of fake news to help understand its dynamics and mitigate its negative impact. Therefore, this study aims to address the gap identified by analysing the fake news stories that were collected during the SA national lockdown, from online platforms such as WhatsApp, Twitter, Facebook and mainstream media related to COVID-19 and to understand the impact caused by creating and sharing fake news.

1.1 Study Context

This study focuses on the proliferation of fake news in SA during which the COVID-19 pandemic was causing severe restrictions and limitations on citizens' lives and mobility.

This continued even after these restrictions were slightly lifted. According to Statistics (Stats) SA mid-year estimates, SA has a population of 59.62 million people [13], of which around 55% of the people have access to the internet and approximately 36% are Facebook subscribers, as of 30 September 2020 [14]. The use of social media platforms continues to increase even during the time of COVID-19. On 5 March 2020, the first COVID-19 case was confirmed in SA. This caused the government to monitor the situation closely. On 15 March 2020, a national lockdown was announced in-order to curb the spread of the virus. This was meant to last for 21 days, but it was extended and later categorised into different alert levels ranging from one to five (five being the most stringent in regulations). With each step down a level, more services, economic sectors, social activities etc. were allowed to operate. With that, people started sharing more information and their views on social media about the pandemic as well as lockdown restrictions. However, some of the stories shared were misleading or fake news, thus leading to this study.

In this paper, we start by giving background information on fake news, theories of fake news as well as fake news on social media in Sect. 2. In Sect. 3, we provide details about the methodology followed to collect, process and verify data. In Sect. 4, we present the analysis and results. In Sect. 5, a discussion is provided which includes findings, limitations and future work; and in Sect. 6, we conclude the study.

2 Related Work

2.1 Fake News

News these days is not only published by journalists but the digital age has allowed almost anyone to share information about current events that are taking place, creating a tremendous information influx which poses a threat to those consuming this information. The term fake news is used interchangeably with other terms such as false information, misinformation, disinformation, inaccurate news, and rumors [14, 15]. All these different terms have a single commonality, i.e. it inhibits good communication and impedes decision-making [16]. Numerous researchers have done work on this subject and each researcher uses a term that best suits what they wish to convey. Duffy [17], described fake news as information that imitates legitimate news but has content that is false and misleading. Wardle and Derakhshan [18] completely avoid using this term and state that it is popularly used by politicians to describe news they disagree with and therefore undermining journalism. Instead, they refer to the term information disorder and introduced a conceptual framework to examine information disorder. They identify three different categories that make up information disorder; misinformation, disinformation and malinformation. These categories are depicted in Fig. 1 with the usage of two dimensions false and harmful.

Despite this, one of the purposes served by fact-checking is to ensure that the true intention of the one who shared information is established by assessing its authenticity and truthfulness [3]. Zhou and Zefari [3], in their study also helped to clarify the fact that no universal definition for fake news exists, which is one of the reasons why numerous definitions exist. Despite this, when fake news is clearly defined in a study it assists in laying a substantial foundation for the analysis of fake news and the evaluation of related studies [3]. Further, a suggestion was made by Egelhofer and Lecheler [19] to differentiate fake news when it comes to its usage to describe disinformation and labels used by politicians to undermine media. Hence, in this research study the term fake news is used and defined as inaccurate or untrue information that is created or disseminated unintentionally or intentionally on social media platforms or websites. In this definition, the dissemination of information might be intentional or unintentional, owing to the fact that some people unknowingly share inaccurate information with the intention to assist others [20].

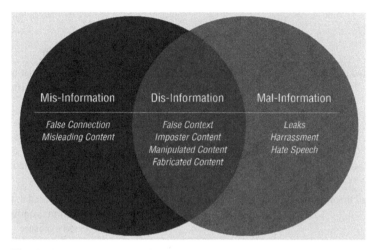

Fig. 1. The Conceptual Framework for examining information disorder [18]

2.2 Theories of Fake News

Theories have been developed by numerous disciplines, e.g. social sciences and economics, which have shown a substantial contribution by providing priceless insights when analysing fake news, and facilitating the construction of well-justified and interpretable models for detecting fake news. In this section, a few theories are listed which can possibly be used when studying fake news. These theories pertain to the news and the users who are spreaders [3].

News-Related Theories. Fake news has been revealed to possess possible characteristics that differ from truthful news, in writing style, quality, word count which is stated by the information manipulation theory and the expressed sentiments which is stated by four-factor theory. Four factor theory was described by Walczyk et al. [21] as an influential theory of deception further stating that deception requires generalised arousal, anxiety, guilt (which is behavior control) and other expressed sentiments to appear truthful. These theories were formulated by forensic psychology and are aimed at deceptive statements but have shared attributes identified in fake news and are therefore pointed out as similar contexts. These are some of the attributes that can be used to detect fake news [3].

User-Related Theories. These theories examine the characteristics of users that participate in fake news activities, for instance posting, sharing, liking and commenting. Fake news perpetrators and normal users can be attracted by fake news, albeit malicious users spread fake news intentionally and are often driven by the benefits they derive [3]. Normal users can unintentionally spread fake news as well, without discerning the falseness of this information. This vulnerability often originates from social impact and self-impact theories such as categorized in Table 1.

Table 1. Table fundamental theories [3].

		Theories	Phenomenon
News-related theories		Information manipulation theory	Extreme information quantity often exists in deception
		Four-factor theory	Lies are expressed differently in terms of arousal. Behavior control, emotion, and thinking from truth
User-related theories	Social Impact	Validity effect	Individuals tend to believe information is correct after repeated exposure
		Bandwagon effect	Individuals do something primarily because others are doing it
	Self-impact	Confirmation bias	Individuals tend to trust information that confirms their preexisting beliefs or hypotheses
		Selective exposure	Individuals prefer information that confirms their preexisting attitudes

In a study conducted by [3], various theories from multiple research studies are depicted, but for the purpose of this study only a few are depicted in Table 1. One of the theories, i.e. validity effect, states that all it takes for one to trust fake news and share unintentionally is the exposure to more fake news spread particularly on social media. Wardle and Derakhsham [18] share similar sentiments and refer to this as a challenge of echo chambers, in most cases when humans are presented with a choice to select who to connect with, we are inclined to build relationships with those that share the same views with us. We then spend a lot of time in echo chambers. Trusting unverified information can also be fortified when fake news confirms preexisting beliefs which is known as confirmation biases and selective bias theories, amongst others, which is also a result of spending time in echo chambers [18]. In this instance when looking from the user's perspective, a strategy to dissolve the spread of fake news should be designed taking into consideration the user's intentions. However, it is difficult to prove someone's intentions especially on social media [18], since people use social media for various reasons, good and bad. For example, removing fake news perpetrators and disabling their accounts is a sensible action to take, but not for normal accounts. Rather, education and availing true news sources can better assist in this regard [3].

2.3 Fake News on Social Media and the Knowledge Gap

Researchers study the topic of fake news in different ways and use cases. Currently, the most prevalent use case includes news about COVID-19 during which a lot of people seek information on social media platforms rather than mainstream media. Hence, efforts have been invested towards studying fake news especially during the time of the COVID-19 pandemic. A study about the connection of social media and fake news during this pandemic era has been conducted by [19, 20]. Frenkel [10] and Russonello [22] shows how the spread of fake news has become more pronounced on social media. A lot of fake news has been shared about COVID-19 and some examples mentioned in literature include preventive cures, how to cope with the virus [9], etc. which presents health risks and undermines the efforts introduced by the government in implementing preventative measures [11]. It is important to note that most of these stories started on social media and were disseminated amongst different users.

With that, different countries started studying the impact and spread of fake news on social media. In Vietnam, a study showed that the spread of fake news exceeds the verified information announced by the government [23]. In Taiwan, numerous posts on social media suggested that the country had witnessed a considerable number of infections and that the Taiwan president was infected, which was later found to be false [10]. In the US, findings on how people failed to reason whether the content is true or false before sharing have been shared and this study further suggests the importance of verifying information before sharing it [9].

In the African context, from the onset of the pandemic, there were misconceptions that the virus would not thrive due to the geographical conditions i.e. temperatures and because Africans have strong immune systems [24]. However, this was debunked by the sudden rise of the virus in the continent which was alarming to those who believed the speculation [20, 25]. A study by Alpert [26] demonstrates the growing number of false information on social media in Nigeria, Kenya, SA, and other African countries. With that, not much research about the impact of fake news in SA has been done or conducted. Most recent studies document comprehensive reports on the virus [27]. Thus, examining the impact of fake news in the context of SA is very crucial to assist in raising awareness on the impact of fake news.

3 Methodology

3.1 Data Collection

This section discusses the different methods and tools employed to collect COVID-19 related data from five online media platforms. The following describes the techniques and the breakdown of the data collected from each platform:

- Mainstream media - One of the tools used was Really Simple Syndication (RSS) feed, a web-based feed that uses a standardised content distribution method to allow users and applications to be up to date with websites. The news outlets (News24, IOL, Daily Maverick, Times Live and The Citizen) that were reporting on COVID-19 were monitored and tracked automatically by the RSS feed that was enabled on the data collector's side. It feeds update notices in real time and links back to the articles reporting on COVID-19.
- Youtube – was not the main platform we focused on. However, we have entries in the dataset from this platform because the video link was shared on either Twitter or Facebook, thus indicating the originator of the data or story shared.
- WhatsApp – It is difficult to collect data from this platform as it is a private platform. Therefore, the data collected in this study (at a very minimal scale) was only collected when data collectors spotted suspicious posts from their WhatsApp contacts. Thus, there is not many details on how data was collected as it was not structured at all.
- Facebook – we manually retrieved relevant data using the keywords listed in Table 2.
- Twitter – Twitter's Application Programming Interface (API) was used to collect data based on the keywords and hashtags defined in Table 2. Twitter is one of the most popular and commonly used social media platforms which allows users to easily communicate with each other and share concerns [26]. This is an observation that was made in this study as well. Hence, it was used for collecting data. Twitter Analytics was used to search for keywords as it allows access to both historical and real-time feeds, and allows one to search or query tweets containing specific keywords or hashtags.

Having the correct keywords for the search on Twitter Analytics was very important, because it produced accurate results. A Tweet Sentiment Visualisation Tool [26] was also used to collect data based on trending hashtags. Some of the constant hashtags were monitored on a daily basis. Table 2 shows some of the popular hashtags and keywords used in SA during the course of the data collection.

To create a dataset, a Google form was used, which allowed data collectors to capture information from the above platforms in various formats i.e., images, text, and links. The dataset was collected over a period of seven months from March 23 to October 30, 2020, certain days were missed i.e. weekends. The study excluded data shared or written in other languages other than English.

Table 2. Popular hashtags and keywords used in SA

Type	Terms
Keywords	Covid19, lockdown, social relief funds, covid19 cases, covid19 tests, coronavirus
Hashtags	#Covid19SA, #Covid19inSA, #CoronavirusInSA, #CoronaVirusSA, #CoronavirusSA, #LockDownSouthAfrica, #COVID19SouthAfrica, #Day[*number since lockdown started*]OfLockDown, #lockdowninsouthafrica, #lockdownextension, 21daysLockdownSA, #SocialDistancing, #StayHomeSA, #endlockdownSA, #Lockdownlevel4, #Covid19fund

3.2 Data Processing

This section describes the techniques undertaken to clean and process the dataset. This was accomplished through the following steps:

- All the data entries were automatically saved in a spreadsheet. There was more than one data collector hence some of the entries were duplicated, as different sources would repeat the same story. Therefore, the removal of duplicates was necessary to obtain unique entries.
- Categorisation of data - this includes assigning each data entry to any of the five categories defined in Table 3. This table was used to distinguish between the categories. It can be noted that a data entry can belong to more than one category.

After processing, the resulting dataset was unique, thus making it easier for it to undergo the analysis process.

Table 3. Defining the categories

Category	Definition	Checklist
Misinformation	Information that is inaccurate or misleading, but the person who is disseminating it believes that it is true and the spread could be unintentional [4]	False context, misleading, mistaken, omissions, satire or parody and no harm intended
Malinformation	Information that is based on reality, but used to inflict harm on a person, organisation or country [18]	Based on reality, false context, hate speech, harassment, deliberate leaks and cause harm
Disinformation	Information that is false, and the person who is disseminating it knows it is false. It is a deliberate, intentional lie, and points to people being actively disinformed by malicious actors [18, 28]	False context, inaccurate, misleading, cause harm, imposter content, manipulated content and fabricated content

(continued)

Table 3. (continued)

Category	Definition	Checklist
Propaganda	Information that tries to influence the emotions, attitudes, opinions and actions of target audiences for political, ideological, and religious purposes through the controlled transmission of deceptive, selectively omitting, and one-sided messages [29, 30]. The intent varies from opinion manipulation and attention redirection to monetisation and traffic attraction [31]	Promoting agenda, harm or support and rumors
Scams	Meant to deceive and defraud someone [32]	False context and defraud

3.3 Data Verification

This section discusses the methods and tools that were employed to verify and debunk fake news spread about COVID-19. All the fake news reported on the pandemic came in different forms, namely: images, videos, articles, chain messages, and posts containing only text. In some incidents, it was very difficult to verify and debunk the authenticity of reported news. For instance, there were cases where images used were modified, altered or recycled and shared across the Internet. In such cases where images were involved, FotoForensics [33] was utilised to analyse these images focusing mainly on the areas where they could have been modified. FotoForensics was started by Dr. Neal Krawitz, a computer scientist, it is a web application that is used widely to detect image manipulation [34]. This tool analyses images and provides details unidentifiable by the human eye, and was used alongside the Google reverse image search tool to discover other similar images that exist on the Internet.

Another issue encountered across social media platforms was a proliferation of fake user accounts. These newly created fake accounts were spreading fake news and causing turmoil across the country. Open source web applications, such as Foller.me [35] were used to analyse fake Twitter accounts. In a study done by Komendantova et al. [36], Foller.me is listed as one of the tools that can be used to counter misinformation. All the fake user accounts were reported and suspended to avoid more fake news on COVID-19 being disseminated.

Virustotal [37], a framework that allows various vendors to contribute with an antivirus engine was used to identify and detect different malwares on websites, and to provide detailed information on non-reputable websites that were reporting any suspicious news. This tool was analysed in a study by Menéndez et al. [38] and was found to be very effective for this purpose. Another technique used on the verification of articles was cross-checking news reports with two or more reputable news outlets including verified fact-checking websites like Africa Check to confirm the authenticity of the news and verify articles and posts containing text. This provided the team with a solid baseline for assessing the news that was reported on various media platforms.

After the verification process which was used to debunk the data in all the categories such as misinformation, disinformation, etc. Some stories were eliminated because of the criteria adopted for verification as well as duplicated stories, thus, a total of 120 unique fake news stories were recorded during the collection period. Numerous stories were duplicated and shared by various sources in various formats, but the main story was the same and in that case, we only recorded it once in the final dataset which trimmed the dataset tremendously.

3.4 Data Annotation

Data annotation is broadly defined as the technique of labelling data (with the aim of enriching textual data) with additional data [39, 40]. The main purpose is to label the data with meaningful classes which will support the process of data analysis [41]. The process of labelling data must be performed repeatedly, which makes up individual annotations [42]. For the purpose of this study, class refers to a department or sector the data entry directly affects. We performed manual verification and labelling of the stories obtained from the data verification step. We employed 3 annotators to label and verify the labels. Each annotator went through the dataset and defined labels by breaking down each story in the dataset to a smaller insightful unit, that they deemed fit for each story as the annotators were familiar with the data and its context. This is also known as the open coding process [43]. Afterwards all appointed annotators went through a step of recontextualisation to check all aspects of the dataset and make sure it covers the aim of the study. They then collated and categorized the dataset according to the labels identified for use. This process was cross checked and repeated to ensure that no inaccuracies existed. After several revisions, 11 departments that were linked to most data entries were identified. These annotations are depicted in Table 4 alongside their definitions and examples, which are referred to as keywords. These annotations aim to assist in determining the impact caused by the dissemination of misinformation to various departments. This technique is similar to a process used in a qualitative study that applies qualitative content analysis [43].

Table 4. Data annotations and definitions.

Department	Keywords	Definition
Education	Schools, Colleges, Universities etc.	All the topics related to lower or higher education
Correctional Services	Correctional service training	Topics related to justice and correctional services
Rural Development and Land Reform	Deeds	Topics related to development and land
Defence	South African National Defence Force (SANDF), soldiers	Topics related to the Defence Force which is responsible for defending South Africa

(continued)

Table 4. (*continued*)

Department	Keywords	Definition
Trade, Industry and Competition	Competition Commission	All the topics related to the competitive economy
Social Development	Relief funds, grants, South African Social Security Agency (SASSA)	Topics related to social transformation, reducing poverty etc.
Health	COVID-19 cases, Personal Protective Equipment (PPEs), COVID-19 vaccines, COVID-19 prevention	All the topics related to the prevention of illnesses, promoting healthy lifestyles and healthcare systems
Miscellaneous	5G technology, China, million body bags, COVID-19 is lab made	All topics that can be classified and can affect different departments i.e. theories about the Gates Foundation, conspiracies, theories about COVID-19 etc
Employment and Labour	Workers	Topics related to reducing unemployment
The Presidency	Lockdown, regulations, lockdown extension, alcohol ban, evictions	All topics related to efforts the government took to curb the spread of COVID-19 i.e. introducing lockdown
South African Police Service (SAPS)	SAPS, Police	Topics related to the police service

4   Analysis

In this section, we analyse the distribution of the collected data to obtain insights on the topics shared, trends, and impact caused. The results on how the identified categories are distributed among various social media platforms are also provided in this section.

The collected data was analysed using descriptive statistics to obtain insight into the following:

- which period was flooded with fake news stories as well as reasons for the flooding at that time.
- which of the identified categories were most prevalent.
- which topics were most prevalent and,
- which social media platforms were the main sources for these stories.

Provided in Fig. 2 are the observations formulated from the analysis of the data.

Figure 2 depicts that the highest peak of fake news stories occurred mostly between 23 March 2020 and 28 May 2020. During this period, more than one story was recorded a day and these stories formed part of all the identified categories described above, with the misinformation category being the most occurring. Regarding the topics, the

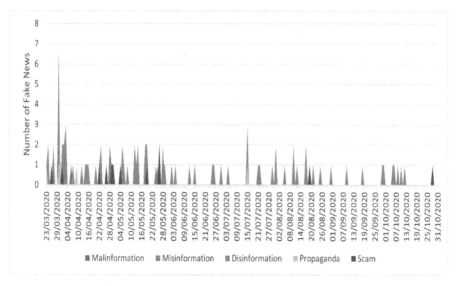

Fig. 2. Number of fake news incidents per fake news category

most occurring stories were around means for treating and curing COVID-19 at home, followed by COVID-19 relief aids offered by the government. The COVID-19 relief aids were meant to assist SA citizens by introducing aids in a form of social grants and food parcels, which led to misinformation around the application process and distributions of food parcels. Between 15 July 2020 to 20 August 2020, another wave of fake news hit (mostly more than one story was recorded a day), though lower than the first one. The stories recorded during this time fell mostly on misinformation and disinformation categories.

Another topic trend was around the education sector as schools closed when the lockdown started and it was unclear as to when they would reopen. Consequently, issues pertaining to the reopening of schools, students repeating same grades in 2021, reopening of other school grades (as the opening of schools was phased in, starting with Grade 12s, 7s and Rs which is the year of schooling before a learner attends Grade 1), consequences of late reopening of schools and the closure of schools again due to the rise of COVID-19 infections became more prevalent. The education sector was not the only sector affected by fake news, a lot of stories were shared about the health sector as well. These stories varied from hospitals recruiting employees, increase of COVID-19 cases in certain hospitals, lack of PPEs. This impacted the health sector, as people started having concerns about the readiness of the sector to fight against the pandemic. Fake news relating to the COVID-19 vaccine introduced vaccine hesitancy, which is delayed acceptance or refusal of the vaccine. Vaccine hesitancy has been a challenge for years towards vaccine preventable diseases like Haemophilus influenzae type b (Hib) [44].

To analyse the impact of misinformation dissemination, annotations were used whereby the stories were categorised by departments. Out of 11 identified annotations, it can be observed that the health sector was impacted the most and was leading at 36.5%, which supports that most prominent topics were around preventing COVID-19 and home remedies for the virus. The second most affected department was The presidency at 21.7%, which in this case focuses on topics related to means put together by the government to curb the spread of COVID-19 i.e. lockdown, and providing assistance to those in need or affected by the pandemic. Depicted in Fig. 3, is the distribution of all the identified annotations.

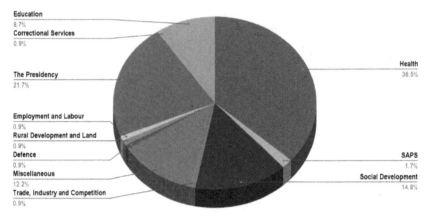

Fig. 3. Distribution of annotations identified

When analysing the sources, it was observed that out of the five sources used for collecting data, most of the data came from Twitter contributing 59%, followed by WhatsApp at 22% and YouTube contributing the least of data at 1%. These results are depicted in Fig. 4.

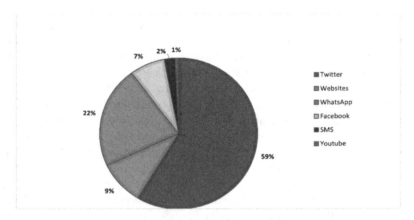

Fig. 4. Percentage of fake news incidents per fake news source

Figure 5 provides insight on how the categorisation of data was distributed among the platforms used for collecting data. It can be observed that Twitter was the main source for three categories, namely: misinformation, malinformation and disinformation. Scams were mainly from WhatsApp followed by Twitter. Twitter and WhatsApp contributed equally in spreading propaganda and were the only sources that spread propaganda.

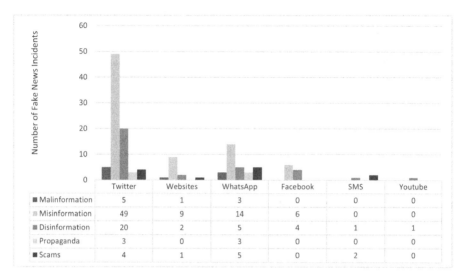

	Twitter	Websites	WhatsApp	Facebook	SMS	Youtube
■ Malinformation	5	1	3	0	0	0
■ Misinformation	49	9	14	6	0	0
■ Disinformation	20	2	5	4	1	1
■ Propaganda	3	0	3	0	0	0
■ Scams	4	1	5	0	2	0

Fig. 5. Source of fake news vs fake news categories

There have been many data visualization projects worldwide around the topic of COVID-19. However, most of them focused mainly on COVID-19 cases including daily

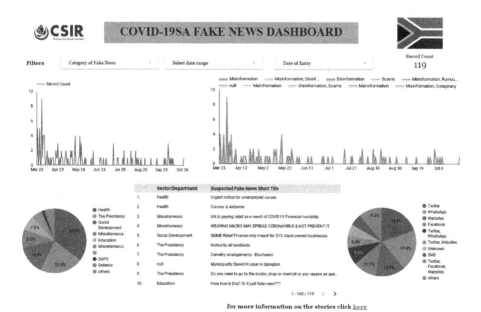

Fig. 6. Confirmed fake news dashboard in SA [37].

increase in reported cases, increase in the number of deaths recorded, mapping where cases are increasing rapidly etc. For this study, a data visualisation dashboard portraying all the confirmed fake news stories was created with the aim to provide easy access and bring awareness to South African citizens. Figure 6 depicts the home page of the dashboard whereby users can search for confirmed fake news stories based on a date or category and it also allows users to filter data based on different filters.

The above section demonstrated how fake news was analysed based on the different factors mentioned. Conclusions were drawn to provide insight on how the spread of fake news can be further monitored and controlled in SA.

5 Discussion

5.1 Findings

The study stems from an observation that was made during the lockdown period as it was quickly realised that there were COVID-19 related fake news circulating across different social media platforms and mainstream media and fake news about the lockdown in general. It was observed that, whenever announcements were made by the President and Government officials regarding lockdown restrictions, fake news would pop up which confused the citizens. This is depicted in Fig. 2. From the results, it was noted that topics about COVID-19 cures and COVID-19 relief aids were largely shared. This caused panic, and more importantly emphasised on lack of health education or awareness, as people were receiving wrong information concerning something vital to their health. This impacted the health sector as people started losing confidence in their capability to fight against the pandemic and introduced vaccine hesitancy. The content of fake news also affected the government aids provided to assist citizens and families during the pandemic. Therefore, people identified opportunities to spread false stories with the intent to scam people on how they can get funds by dialing a certain number or providing their confidential banking details. From the results it is clear that most of the scams were mainly from WhatsApp as it is easier for users to make voice calls or send messages since most of the scams require users to reply via text. The general public was vulnerable during this period, and so it became easier to mislead them. Overall, it can be observed that, in SA social media especially Twitter is the largest contributor of fake news. A lot of articles exist about the spread of fake news via social media and SA is catching up, but there is a need for awareness and more research pertaining to reasons behind people spreading fake news during such a time. Social media makes it particularly easy to spread fake news because of the wide audience, but also the lack of substantial filtering of posts from a third-party, there is little to no fact-checking or even editorial judgement so people are free to share any information [38]. As the lockdown period progressed, more stories were shared depending on the popular topics discussed in the country.

The education sector was also impacted as there was a lot of discomfort about pupils and students going back to school in the middle of a pandemic. The government took time deciding on the course of action when it came to the curriculum because there were adverse consequences to missing school, such as interrupted learning and missing out on education. Thus, fake news emerged about the closing and reopening of schools. This caused panic among those affected, as they did not know what was true or false at this point. The sharing of fake news during the social media era is a great concern because it allows users to hide their real identity, write freely without being vetted, and their geographical location is not always known [39].

5.2 Limitations and Future Work

Even though the study was a success, it was not without limitations and this section highlights some of the limitations that were encountered. Firstly, the study excludes any data that is not published in English (there are 11 official languages in SA) which means there were omissions of relevant information published in other languages. Secondly, there is an incomplete representation of the populace, as the study only focuses on social media platforms which are not used as often especially in rural areas, thus limiting the sample size. Thirdly, the difficulty of collecting real-time social media data which can enable timely assessment of public reactions to opinions, epidemic control measures, and the timely clarification of rumors. This leads to the difficulty in capturing a story's originator which results in finding the story when a government or department official account or website has confirmed that the story is fake. Lastly, limited resources were also a constraint in verifying the authenticity of the news. With technology rapidly evolving, there is so much one can do in verifying sources of the news. To some extent, it becomes difficult to stay updated with the evolution of media platforms, this results in having a few limited technologies at your disposal to monitor and verify the news.

There are several directions for future work to address this large-scale infodemic surrounding COVID-19 in SA. Firstly, to improve fake news detection by having an automated process for collecting data. Secondly, to conduct a sentiment analysis (to understand people's behavior and intentions when sharing fake news), which would provide insights for future cases. Lastly, to analyse how algorithmic correction can be utilized by a platform (i.e. social media platform like Twitter) and by users for correction.

6 Conclusion

In this paper, an exploratory study that analyses the impact of sharing fake news during the COVID-19 pandemic is presented. Despite the vast reviews of literature presented so far, nothing much has been studied in the case of SA. This is evident from the literature study, which goes into depth about the theories of fake news, and fake news on social media. Although this study explains the impact of fake news, it is limited by its ability to empirically explain the causes and effects of fake news proliferation. The methodology followed to collect, process, verify and analyse data, has been provided.

The data collected and analysed for this study is over a period of seven months. From the beginning of the study, it can be noted that the spread of fake news in SA was high and there was a lack of awareness since the exposure to fake news is often overlooked by people. However, towards the end of the data collection period, the records of fake news decreased tremendously as the government invested time to raise awareness about the impact of fake news. With that said, efforts still need to be invested in educating people, raising awareness about fake news, and coming up with strategies for the future.

The findings detailed in this study can assist the government in developing successful interventions in the future.

The analysis shows that Twitter is the leading platform used to disseminate fake news at 59% followed by WhatsApp at 22%. From this, it is evident that in the South African context, people tend to use Twitter the most to share their concerns and this can be leveraged in the future. Thus, this provides insights, i.e. knowledge on which platforms to focus on during a pandemic or to curb the spread of fake news and these findings can assist the government and other organisations in developing successful interventions and coming up with strategies in the future.

References

1. Knowledge@Wharton: "The Impact of Social Media: Is it Irreplaceable?" 26 July 2019. https://knowledge.wharton.upenn.edu/article/impact-of-social-media/. Accessed 18 Nov 2020
2. Hudson, M.: What Is Social Media? Definition and Examples of Social Media, 23 June 2020. https://www.thebalancesmb.com/what-is-social-media-2890301
3. Zhou, X., Zafarani, R.: A survey of fake news: fundamental theories, detection methods, and opportunities. ACM Comput. Surv. **53**(5), 1–40 (2020). https://doi.org/10.1145/3395046
4. Lazer, D.M.J., et al.: The science of fake news. Science (80-.). **359**(6380), 1094–1096 (2018). https://doi.org/10.1126/science.aao2998
5. Gottfried, J., Shearer, E.: News Use Across Social Media Platforms 2016, 26 MAY 2016. https://www.journalism.org/2016/05/26/news-use-across-social-media-platforms-2016/
6. WHO: WHO Director-General's opening remarks at the media briefing on COVID-19, 30 November 2020. https://www.who.int/director-general/speeches/detail/who-director-general-s-opening-remarks-at-the-media-briefing-on-covid-19---30-november-2020
7. Cucinotta, D., Vanelli, M.: WHO Declares COVID-19 a Pandemic, 19 March 2020. https://pubmed.ncbi.nlm.nih.gov/32191675/. Accessed 17 Nov 2020
8. Zarocostas, J.: How to fight an infodemic. Lancet (Lond. Engl.) **395**(10225), 676 (2020). https://doi.org/10.1016/S0140-6736(20)30461-X
9. Pennycook, G., McPhetres, J., Zhang, Y., Lu, J.G., Rand, D.G.: Fighting COVID-19 misinformation on social media: experimental evidence for a scalable accuracy-nudge intervention. Psychol. Sci. **31**(7), 770–780 (2020). https://doi.org/10.1177/0956797620939054
10. Frenkel, S., Alba, D., Zhong, R.: Surge of Virus Misinformation Stumps Facebook and Twitter. The New York Times (2020). https://www.nytimes.com/2020/03/08/technology/coronavirus-misinformation-social-media.html
11. Lampos, V., et al.: Tracking COVID-19 using online search, no. July 2020. http://arxiv.org/abs/2003.08086
12. Pulido, C.M., Ruiz-Eugenio, L., Redondo-Sama, G., Villarejo-Carballido, B.: A new application of social impact in social media for overcoming fake news in health. Int. J. Environ. Res. Public Health **17**(7), 2430 (2020). https://doi.org/10.3390/ijerph17072430
13. Statistics South Africa. Mid-year population estimates 2020. Statistical Release P0302. [online] Pretoria: Statistics South Africa, pp. 8–9 (2021). http://www.statssa.gov.za/publications/P0302/P03022020.pdf
14. Miniwatts Marketing Group: "Internet Users Statistics for Africa (Africa Internet Usage, 2020 Population Stats and Facebook Subscribers)", 12 November 2020. https://www.internetworldstats.com/stats1.htm. Accessed 30 Nov 2020
15. Al-Zaman, M.S.: COVID-19-related fake news in social media. SSRN Electron. J. 1–12 (2020). https://doi.org/10.2139/ssrn.3644107

16. Memon, S.A., Carley, K.M.: Characterizing COVID-19 misinformation communities using a novel twitter dataset. In: CEUR Workshop Proceedings, vol. 2699 (2020)
17. Duffy, A., Tandoc, E., Ling, R.: Too good to be true, too good not to share: the social utility of fake news. Inf. Commun. Soc. **23**(13), 1965–1979 (2020). https://doi.org/10.1080/1369118X.2019.1623904
18. Wardle, C., Derakhshan, H.: Thinking about 'information disorder': formats of misinformation, disinformation, and mal-information. J. "fake news" disinformation-UNESCO 43–54 (2018). https://en.unesco.org/sites/default/files/f._jfnd_handbook_module_2.pdf
19. Egelhofer, J.L., Lecheler, S.: Fake news as a two-dimensional phenomenon: a framework and research agenda. Ann. Int. Commun. Assoc. **43**(2), 97–116 (2019). https://doi.org/10.1080/23808985.2019.1602782
20. Apuke, O.D., Omar, B.: Fake news and COVID-19: modelling the predictors of fake news sharing among social media users. Telemat. Inform. **56**(July 2020), 101475 (2021). https://doi.org/10.1016/j.tele.2020.101475
21. Walczyk, J.J., Igou, F.P., Dixon, A.P., Tcholakian, T.: Advancing lie detection by inducing cognitive load on liars: a review of relevant theories and techniques guided by lessons from polygraph-based approaches. Front. Psychol. **4**(February), 1–13 (2013). https://doi.org/10.3389/fpsyg.2013.00014
22. Russonello, G.: Afraid of Coronavirus? That Might Say Something About Your Politics, The New York Times (2020). https://www.nytimes.com/2020/03/13/us/politics/coronavirus-trump-polling.html
23. Huynh, T.L.D.: The COVID-19 risk perception: a survey on socioeconomics and media attention. Econ. Bull. **40**(1), 1–8 (2020)
24. Ryder, H.: AFRICA ONLOOKS COVID-19 is only slowly reaching Africa. That's no surprise. The Africa Report (2020). https://www.theafricareport.com/24160/covid-19-is-only-slowly-reaching-africa-thats-no-surprise/
25. Ahinkorah, B.O., Ameyaw, E.K., Hagan, J.E., Seidu, A.-A., Schack, T.: Rising above misinformation or fake news in Africa: another strategy to control COVID-19 spread. Front. Commun. **5**(June), 2018–2021 (2020). https://doi.org/10.3389/fcomm.2020.00045
26. Alpert, L.I.: Coronavirus misinformation spreads on Facebook. Watchdog Says, 20 April 2020. https://www.wsj.com/articles/coronavirus-misinformation-spreads-on-facebook-watchdog-says-11587436159
27. Sahu, K.K., Mishra, A.K., Lal, A.: Comprehensive update on current outbreak of novel coronavirus infection (2019-nCoV). Ann. Transl. Med. **8**(6), 393 (2020). https://doi.org/10.21037/atm.2020.02.92
28. Karlova, N., Fisher, K.: A social diffusion model of misinformation and disinformation for understanding human information behavior. Inf. Res. **18**(1), 4 (2013). http://informationr.net/ir/18-1/paper573.html#.YAqh7-gzZPY
29. Volkova, S., Jang, J.Y.: Misleading or falsification: inferring deceptive strategies and types in online news and social media. In: Web Conference 2018 - Companion World Wide Web Conference WWW 2018, pp. 575–583 (2018). https://doi.org/10.1145/3184558.3188728
30. Pierri, F., Ceri, S.: False news on social media: a data-driven survey. SIGMOD Rec. **48**(2), 18–32 (2019). https://doi.org/10.1145/3377330.3377334
31. Volkova, S., Shaffer, K., Jang, J.Y., Hodas, N.: Separating facts from fiction: linguistic models to classify suspicious and trusted news posts on twitter. In: ACL 2017 - Proceedings of the 55th Annual Meeting of the Association for Computational Linguistics (Long Papers), vol. 2, pp. 647–653 (2017). https://doi.org/10.18653/v1/P17-2102
32. "Merriam-Webster," (2021). https://www.merriam-webster.com/dictionary/scams
33. "Fotoforensics," (2021). http://fotoforensics.com/

34. Beck, T.S.: How to Detect Image Manipulations Part I - Error Level Analysis in Practice. HEADT Centre (2017). https://headt.eu/How-to-Detect-Image-Manipulations-Part-1. Accessed 20 Jan 2007
35. "Twitter Analytics" (2021). https://foller.me/
36. Komendantova, N., et al.: A value-driven approach to addressing misinformation in social media. Humanit. Soc. Sci. Commun. **8**(1), 1–12(2021). https://doi.org/10.1057/s41599-020-00702-9
37. "Virustotal" (2021). https://www.virustotal.com/
38. Menéndez, H.D., Clark, D., Barr, E.T.: Getting ahead of the arms race: hothousing the coevolution of virustotal with a packer. Entropy **23**(4), 1–19 (2021). https://doi.org/10.3390/e23040395
39. Bloomberg, A.S., Tseng, T., Analyst, L., Law, B., Stent, A., Maida, D.: Best Practices for Managing Data Annotation Projects Best Practices for Managing Data Annotation Projects Chief Data Officer, Global Data Best Practices for Managing Data Annotation Projects, no. September, pp. 1–34 (2020). https://www.researchgate.net/publication/344343972
40. Pagel, J., Reiter, N., Rösiger, I., Schulz, S.: A unified text annotation workflow for diverse goals. In: CEUR Workshop Proceedings, vol. 2155, pp. 31–36 (2018)
41. Schreiner, C., Torkkola, K., Gardner, M., Zhang, K.: Using machine learning techniques to reduce data annotation time. In: Proceedings of the Human Factors and Ergonomics Society Annual Meeting, no. October, pp. 2438–2442 (2006). https://doi.org/10.1177/154193120605002219
42. Pick, S., Weyers, B., Hentschel, B., Kuhlen, T.W.: Design and evaluation of data annotation workflows for cave-like virtual environments. IEEE Trans. Vis. Comput. Graph. **22**(4), 1452–1461 (2016). https://doi.org/10.1109/TVCG.2016.2518086
43. Bengtsson, M.: How to plan and perform a qualitative study using content analysis. NursingPlus Open **2**, 8–14 (2016). https://doi.org/10.1016/j.npls.2016.01.001
44. Samal, J.: Impact of COVID-19 infodemic on psychological wellbeing and vaccine hesitancy. Egypt. J. Bronchol. **15**(1), 1–6 (2021). https://doi.org/10.1186/s43168-021-00061-2

A Study of Misinformation in Audio Messages Shared in WhatsApp Groups

Alexandre Maros[1]([✉]), Jussara M. Almeida[1], and Marisa Vasconcelos[2]

[1] Universidade Federal de Minas Gerais, Belo Horizonte, Brazil
{alexandremaros,jussara}@dcc.ufmg.br
[2] IBM Research, São Paulo, Brazil
marisaav@br.ibm.com

Abstract. Recent studies have shown that group communication on WhatsApp plays a significant role to foster information dissemination at large, with evidence of its use for misinformation campaigns. We analyze more than 40K audio messages shared in over 364 publicly accessible groups in Brazil, covering six months of great social mobilization in the country. We identify the presence of misinformation in these audios by relying on previously checked facts. Our study focuses on content and propagation properties of audio misinformation, contrasting them with unchecked content as well as with prior findings of misinformation in other media types. We also rely on a set of volunteers to perform a qualitative analysis of the audios. We observed that audios with misinformation had a higher presence of negative emotions and also often used phrases in the future tense and talked directly to the listener. Moreover, audios with misinformation tend to spread quicker than unchecked content and last significantly longer in the network. The speaker's tone from the audios with misinformation was also considered less *friendly* and *natural* than the unchecked ones. Our study contributes to the literature by focusing on a media type that is gaining mainstream popularity recently, and, as we show here, is being used as vessel for misinformation spread.

Keywords: WhatsApp · Audio messages · Misinformation

1 Introduction

WhatsApp has become a major communication platform worldwide. In fact, as of January 2021, two billion users were accessing the messenger app on a monthly basis[1], surpassing, by far, the monthly usage of other popular platforms such as Facebook Messenger, Telegram, and Snapchat. The app stands out for offering a simple and easy-to-use set of features that allows anyone to quickly share texts, images, audios, videos, or files with individual users or several people at once, through the so-called group communication.

---

[1] www.statista.com/statistics/258749/most-popular-global-mobile-messenger-apps.

© Springer Nature Switzerland AG 2021
J. Bright et al. (Eds.): MISDOOM 2021, LNCS 12887, pp. 85–100, 2021.
https://doi.org/10.1007/978-3-030-87031-7_6

The widespread use of WhatsApp motivated several studies on different aspects of the platform [7, 13, 15, 18, 20–22]. Most studies exploited the fact that, though private spaces by default, WhatsApp groups can be made publicly accessible as group managers share invitation links in public websites. By clicking on those links and joining these publicly accessible groups, researchers were able to gather data for further analysis. These studies showed that WhatsApp is not a mere communication tool but rather exhibits characteristics of social networks like Facebook, and Reddit, with the emergence of robust networks interconnecting users which facilitate the quick spread of information [18, 22]. With a particular focus on the misuse of the platform for spreading fake content, some authors analyzed content properties and general propagation dynamics of misinformation shared in WhatsApp groups, aiming at identifying distinctive properties of this type of content in image [22] and textual [21] messages.

However, online users in general, and WhatsApp users in particular [9], have been showing a growing interest in *audio* content. On one hand, neither text nor image messaging can fully convey the sender's tone, urgency, emotion, or purpose [23] as audio content can, and some prior studies relied on audio media to capture these peculiarities [8]. As such, audio conversations may lead to fewer misinterpretations than textual content. On the other, sharing audio content can be more convenient, especially for the sender. Unfortunately, the increase in popularity of audio messages on WhatsApp has been followed by reports on the use of this type of media as an effective vessel to spread misinformation on the platform[2]. Indeed, in a preliminary analysis of audio messages shared in publicly accessible WhatsApp groups in Brazil, we showed some initial evidence of the presence of audios with previously checked fake content [13].

We build on our prior work [13], focused mostly on developing a methodology to analyze audio content gathered from WhatsApp groups. Following the evidence raised in that work, we here delve into WhatsApp audio messages, offering what we believe to be *the first analysis of the spread of misinformation in audio messages*. Specifically, we aim to tackle the following research questions (RQs):

RQ1: What are the characteristics of audio messages with misinformation shared in publicly accessible WhatsApp groups in terms of content properties and propagation dynamics? How do they compare to prior findings of misinformation in other media types on the platform [21, 22]?

RQ2: How do the content and dynamics properties of audio messages carrying previously checked misinformation compare with the properties of the other audio messages?

To address these questions, we rely on a dataset obtained from [22], consisting of over 43 thousand messages collected from *publicly accessible* and *politically-oriented* WhatsApp groups in Brazil. Our study relies on qualitative and quantitative analyses to unveil content and propagation properties of misinformation in audio, comparing them against similar properties of unchecked audio messages as well as properties of misinformation in other media types reported in [21, 22].

---

[2] https://www.politico.com/news/2020/03/16/coronavirus-fake-news-pandemic-133 447.

Our main findings reveal that audio communication is widely used in the 364 monitored WhatsApp groups, with more than 42 thousand audio messages across six months. Based on the misinformation detection, we marked over 120 unique audios that were shared more than 2,000 times across 260 groups during the monitored period. We observed that audios with misinformation appear in more groups and are shared by more users than their counterparts. Lastly, we noticed many particular characteristics that emerged more often in audios with misinformation, such as a call to action (actively asking the listener to take some action, such as share the audio) and being more related to negative emotions.

This paper is organized as follows. Section 2 presents related work. Section 3 describes our methodology to analyze audio content share on WhatsApp groups, notably how we identified audios containing misinformation. Our analyses on content properties, including the results of a qualitative investigation, are presented in Sect. 4, whereas results on propagation dynamics are discussed in Sect. 5. Conclusions and future work are offered in Sect. 6.

2   Related Work

Recent studies investigated the dissemination of misinformation on social media platforms. Since the 2016 U.S. presidential election, the spread of misinformation is increasing around the world. The so-called fake news may contribute to political polarization, decrease trust in public institutions, and lead people to have less faith in the political process. Social media bots on Twitter were observed during the 2016 U.S. Presidential election [3]. Out of almost 3 million distinct users involved in political discussions, 400 thousand were bots being responsible for 3.8 million tweets (one-fifth of all collected tweets). These numbers are worrisome since these bots can act in an orchestrated way to influence and promote discussion, impulsing content with misinformation, and influencing what is being discussed by real users [1]. Bots are not only targeting politics, but also several other areas, such as debates regarding vaccination campaigns [5], and are present in several social networks [10].

Recently, a few studies have looked into user behavior and content dissemination in WhatsApp groups. Garimella *et al.* [11,14] proposed a general data collection methodology for collecting Whatsapp public groups and analyzed misinformation in images shared groups in India. Josemar *et al.* [7] analyzed political and non-political groups using cascade model as well as dissemination of misinformation. They observe that cascades with misinformation tend to be deeper, reach more users, and last longer in political groups than in non-political ones. Bursztyn *et al.* [6] focus on understanding the differences between right and left-wing Whatsapp groups during the 2018 Brazilian Presidential election. They found that right-wing groups are more abundant, tightly connected, and geographically distributed, while also sharing more multimedia messages. Melo *et al.* [15] evaluate the dynamics of the spread of misinformation in WhatsApp groups. Using an epidemiological model, the authors showed how the forwarding feature contributes to the content virality, and why system limitations are not effective to prevent a message to reach the entire network quickly. Resende *et al.* [22] studied the types of content shared in publicly accessible WhatsApp groups during two events in 2018 in Brazil. The authors proposed a method to identify misinformation in images shared across the groups. They found that images with previously checked misinformation tend to be reshared within shorter intervals and are more often shared first on WhatsApp and then on the Web. Later, the same authors extended their prior work by focusing on shared textual messages [21]. The analysis of psychological elements in the text showed a frequent presence of the insight category in messages with misinformation, often used in chain messages. In terms of propagation dynamics, textual messages are shared more times, by a larger number of users and in more groups. The ones containing misinformation tend to spread faster within particular groups, but take longer to propagate across different groups.

Lastly, our preliminary work [13] focused on studying **audio messages** in WhatsApp, going over a basic content analysis of all audio messages as well as some evidence on misinformation in audio messages. We build on this prior work and focus on identifying the differences of audio messages with misinformation versus unchecked content.

3   Methodology

In this section we describe the methodology we employed in our study, focusing particularly on the WhatsApp dataset used. We briefly review how we gathered and processed the dataset, following steps described in detail in [13]. We also present how we identified misinformation in the audio messages collected.

3.1   WhatsApp Dataset

This work relies on the same raw dataset collected in [21,22], which contains messages collected from publicly accessible WhatsApp groups from 21st of May to 28th of October of 2018. Those studies focused on analyzing messages containing textual and image content only. More recently, we complemented those studies by looking into audio messages, offering a preliminary analysis of content properties, audio type (music vs. speech) and propagation dynamics [13].

To that end, we employed a multi-step methodology to process the audio content collected, consisting of (i) pre-processing, to guarantee that all audios are in the same format; (ii) similarity detection, to group audios that have similar content together; and (iii) speech recognition phase to transcribe the audios, allowing for the use of natural language processing tools to analyze their content. Very briefly, to identify and group audios with similar content, we employed the open-source library called Chromaprint[3], which processes and transforms the audio frequency in musical notes and uses this new representation to compare different files. Using the fingerprints produced by Chromprint, we performed a

---

[3] https://acoustid.org/chromaprint.

pairwise comparison of audios, grouping as "similar" (or near-duplicates), audio pairs for which Chromaprint returned a score of similarity above a given threshold, which was selected after a manual investigation of a sample of audios pairs. For each group of near-duplicates, we elected one audio as representative of the content. Moreover, to be able to analyze that content, we used Google's Speech-to-Text API[4] to produce a transcription of each (unique) audio content. This API returns a score of confidence on the transcription produced. Based on a manual evaluation, we selected a threshold of confidence of 0.8, only keeping transcriptions whose confidence exceeded this defined threshold. In this phase, we also filter audios that were not in Portuguese, as those yields a low confidence threshold since the API is set to Portuguese. We refer the reader to [13] to a detailed description of how these steps were performed.

Table 1. Dataset overview (* users and groups with at least one audio message).

	Truck drivers' strike	Election campaign	Whole collected period
# Groups	117	330	364
# Users*	1,134	6,002	8,056
# Audio message	5,780	28,593	42,869
# Unique audios	1,450	8,505	16,503
# Transcripted audios	987	5,913	11,700

Table 1 shows overall statistics about the dataset for the whole period of analysis, as well as for each of the two selected periods separately, the national truck drivers' strike (between May 21st and June 2nd) and the general election campaign in Brazil (from August 16th to October 28th). It shows the total number of audio messages shared, the total number of users who shared at least one audio, and groups where at least one audio was shared. Overall, we have more than 8 thousand different users who shared almost 43 thousand audio files in 364 different groups. The table also shows the total number of unique audio contents as well as the number of unique audios for which a transcription with enough confidence was obtained, identified following the methodology described above. The latter, corresponding to around 71% of all audios, was indeed the content used in our analysis. We note that the same audio content was shared 3–4 times on average. However, as we will see later, some audio contents were shared a much larger number of times.

3.2 Misinformation Detection

We expand the methodology developed in [13] by adding a fourth step: misinformation detection. Detecting misinformation is a challenging task. Prior efforts relied on various strategies, including the use of fuzzy analytic hierarchy process [2] and the detection of social bots as an initial step for computation fact-checking

---

[4] https://cloud.google.com/speech-to-text/.

[16]. Another approach is by relying on fact-checking journalists and agencies, which are experts in assessing the truth of a public claim by seeking reliable sources, analyzing facts, images, and videos as well as directly contacting those involved in these claims [12].

Following prior analyses of misinformation in textual and image content on WhatsApp [21,22], we here chose to rely on fact-checking agencies to find misinformation in the content of the audios in our dataset. We used a dataset containing a list of fact-checked claims, made available by [22], gathered from 6 important fact-checking agencies sites in Brazil. We identified audios with misinformation by comparing each audio transcription in our dataset with a fact-checked claim marked as containing misinformation by at least one of the fact-checking agencies. Specifically, we first pre-processed all audio transcriptions and checked-as-fake claims by removing stopwords and using lemmatization. Next, we represented each transcription and checked-as-fake claim by a TF-IDF vector [17]. Then, we calculated the similarity of each audio transcription a with a checked-as-fake claim b by computing the cosine similarity between the corresponding TF-IDF vectors. We did that for each pair (a, b) of transcription a and checked-as-fake claim b.

We manually analyzed the 300 pairs of texts (audio transcription and checked-as-fake claims) with the highest cosine similarity. Our goal was to assess whether the audio transcription contained the same content as the previously checked fake claim. As per the manual analysis, we found that only 100 out of the 300 transcriptions analyzed indeed carried the same content as the claim they were matched to with the highest similarity. These audios were marked as containing misinformation[5], and are the focus of our analyses in the following sections. All other 200 audio messages, as well as all other audios with lower similarity compared to the collected claims, were marked as *unchecked*. We use the term unchecked to emphasize that all we can state is that they are not similar to any previously checked-as-fake claim collected. Thus, strictly speaking, they might or might not carry misinformation. However, we do expect that we were able to catch most audio messages containing misinformation in our dataset, especially those with greater impact on users, as they most probably were reported by at least one of the fact-checkers. As future work, we intend to explore other text similarity methods such as word embeddings.

4 Content Analysis

We now analyze the content of the audios shared, distinguishing between audios with misinformation and unchecked content. To that end, we focus on the audio transcriptions. We start by uncovering the main topics of discussion conveyed in each set of shared audios, and then we look into some psychological linguistic features extracted from their transcriptions. Next, we rely on volunteers to offer a qualitative analysis of the content of a sample of audios.

---

[5] These 100 audios represent distinct content that was shared during the period of analysis. As we will see, each content was indeed shared multiple times.

Table 2. Most representative words for each topic inferred by LDA method

Topic	Most representative words
1	Brazil, Country, Person, Brazilian, Politician, Year, PT, Family, Govern, Defend
2	Expensive, Talk, Stay, See, Understand, Marry, End, Impose, Woman, Nobody
3	Federal, Public, Congressperson, Million, Lula, Paulo, Money, Year, Candidate, Politician
4	Military, Brazil, Stop, Truck Driver, Army, World, Brazilian, Military intervention
5	Bolsonaro, Vote, Brazil, Haddad, PT, President, Jair, Election
6	God, Lord, Jesus, Life, Word, Day, Love, Heart, Father, Name
7	Guys, People, Talk, Understand, Stay, Do, Happen, Find
8	Day, Hour, Guys, City, Car, Night, Today, Come, Friend

4.1 Topic Analysis

To infer the topics conveyed by the audio messages, we employed the Latent Dirichlet Allocation (LDA) algorithm [4] on our collection of audio transcriptions. LDA receives as input all audio transcriptions and the desired number of topics k, and it computes the topic distribution, which can be interpreted as k clusters, each one represented by a word distribution. Words with higher weights in this distribution are more representative of the given topic, thus for each input audio transcript, we can infer the most related topic.

We pre-processed all the transcriptions by removing punctuation marks and stopwords, lowercasing, and stemming all the words.

As a next step, we used all the (pre-processed) transcriptions as input to the LDA model. We used the LDA implementation provided by Gensim[6], a Python library that implements LDA algorithm. Based on this, we obtain the words associated with the k topics learned by the model, and with those words, we can get a better understanding of what is discussed in each topic. To select the best number of topics k, we ran the algorithm varying the number of topics k from 2 to 20 and assessed the quality of the results, measuring the topic coherence c_v. We found the best topic coherence at $k = 8$ topics.

Table 2 presents the top-10 most representative words of each topic. Note that topics 1, 3, and 5 are closely related to politics since they are characterized by words such as "Campaign", "Brazil", "Mayor", "Politician", "PT" (an important political party in the country) and so on. Topic 4 is closely related to the truck drivers' strike event, identified by the words "Trucks", "Truck Driver" and "Military Intervention" (a topic largely discussed during the truck driver's strike). Topic 6 contains mostly words related to religion, suggesting that many audios were recordings of members of Christian denominations members. Finally, topics 2, 7–8 are more loosely connected and encompass more general narratives.

To analyze the distribution of topics across different audio transcriptions, we first assigned to each transcription the most prevalent topic according to LDA

---

[6] https://radimrehurek.com/gensim/.

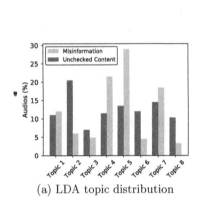
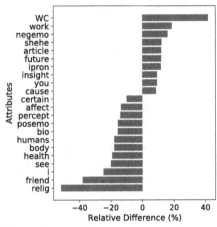

(a) LDA topic distribution

(b)   Relative difference in prevalence of LIWC attributes between misinformation and unchecked

Fig. 1. Content properties of audios with misinformation and with unchecked ones.

results, i.e., the topic with the highest probability associated with the transcription. Figure 1a presents the distributions of topics across different transcriptions, separately considering audios with misinformation and unchecked ones. Note that 52% of audios with misinformation are characterized as containing content related to topics 4 and 5, which are the most strongly related topics to the social mobilization events that happened in the period – the truck drivers' strike and the elections. These two topics are characterized by words such as "Military", "Truck Driver", and "Election". Topic 7 is the third most predominant topic among audios containing misinformation: 18% of them are characterized by this topic which covers words such as "Guys" and "Do". Unchecked audios are more equally distributed across all topics. The topic that holds the largest fraction of audios with unchecked content is Topic 2, which is characterized by words like "Understand" and "Talk", with almost 21% of audios falling into this category.

4.2   Psychological Linguistic Features

We also analyzed the psycholinguistic properties of the audio transcriptions using the 2015 Linguistic Inquiry and Word Count (LIWC) lexicon [19]. LIWC that categorizes words into linguistic style, affective and cognitive attributes. We ran each audio transcription through the Portuguese version of LIWC[7], computing the distributions of each LIWC attribute among audios that were marked as containing misinformation as well as the audios with unchecked content. For each LIWC attribute, we compared the two distributions to identify

---

[7] Provided by http://143.107.183.175:21380/portlex/index.php/pt/projetos/liwc.

which attributes were significantly different across the two sets of audio messages. To compare each pair of distributions, we use the Kolmogorov-Smirnov test, selecting attributes that had a p-value < 0.05 as significantly different.

Aiming at contrasting the most common LIWC attributes in audio transcriptions classified as misinformation and transcriptions containing previously unchecked content, we computed, for each LIWC attribute that was marked as being significantly different in the two types of messages, the ratio of the difference between the values of the attribute in audios with misinformation and audios with unchecked content to the value of the attribute in audios with unchecked content. This ratio implies how much more prevalent, percent-wise, the attribute is among audios with misinformation, compared to audios with unchecked content. Positive ratios imply that the attribute is more present in audios with misinformation, whereas negative ratios mean a greater prevalence among unchecked content.

Figure 1b shows the relative differences for attributes identified as significantly different across the two sets of audios. We note that audios with misinformation tend to be longer, with a higher word count (WC). Furthermore, messages with misinformation tend to be more related to work, characterized by words such as jobs and employment, have more negative emotions (e.g., "hate", "ugly"), use words from the third person singular, such as "she" and "he", carry phrases in the future tense and have words related to insights, such as "think" and "know". Moreover, audios with misinformation also tend to use words such as "you" or "your" (e.g., "it is your problem") and use words related to causation, such as "because" and "to that effect". In contrast, messages with previously unchecked content tend to carry more positive emotions, use the first person singular and cover words related to health, religion and friendship. These observations point towards a clear distinction in discourse in the misinformation audios. Interestingly, when comparing these results with those obtained for textual messages [21], we notice that in both audio and textual messages, there is the predominance of the insight attribute on misinformation. However, in textual messages, words such as "we" and "they" appear more frequently in misinformation, which is not the case here, with "you" being more frequent. Textual messages with misinformation also had a high presence of the sexual attribute, however we found no significant presence of this attribute in audio messages with misinformation. Lastly, textual messages also tend to be associated with the present, whereas audios are more often associated with the future tense.

4.3   Qualitative Analysis

To delve deeper into the content of the audios, we conducted a qualitative analysis of a sample of 100 audios by volunteers. The study is composed of two phases: an interview and a survey. The goal of the interview was to gather the perceptions of selected volunteers on the audios' content with a limited number of audios and use the insights to develop an online survey to reach a broader public.

First Phase: Interview. We interviewed three volunteers separately, with each interview consisting of a one-hour online session, using a semi-structured format, with a defined list of questions to be answered by the volunteers. Each volunteer filled a consent form to allow the use of their responses in this study in an anonymous format. Each interview can be divided into two phases. The first phase consists of questions aimed at learning more about the volunteers, their participation in WhatsApp groups, and their perception of audio in general. During the second phase, the volunteers were asked to listen to four randomly selected audio files. After each audio, they were asked to answer questions regarding their perception of it. Out of the four audios, two contained misinformation, and two had unchecked content.

Regarding the volunteers' perception of the listened audios, we analyzed their answers separately for audios with misinformation and audios with unchecked content. Audios with misinformation were spotted easily as potential sources of misinformation, possibly due to the volunteers' close familiarity with studies on misinformation[8]. In some cases, they also reported finding a certain tone of artificiality in the tone of the speakers of these audios. The volunteers often pointed out that often the speaker of audios with misinformation tried to create a link with someone important as a strategy to bring credibility to the information being transmitted (e.g., the speaker was related to a famous newscaster) as well as trying to back their claims with sources. The volunteers also noted that audios with misinformation tried to engage more with the listener, often trying to create the illusion of familiarity and intimacy, referring to the listener by terms that relate to friendship or family. Overall, we noticed some peculiarities common in audios with misinformation, such as the feeling of uneasiness and the use of strategies to engage more with the public. With these peculiarities mapped out, we moved into the second part of the analysis to identify whether these characteristics were frequent.

Second Phase: Online Survey. Based on the insights collected in the interview, we set up an online survey to gather more information on differences between audios with misinformation and unchecked content. We also wanted to check whether the previous remarks collected were also noticed by a larger group on a broad set of audios. The online form is composed of two sets of questions, one related to volunteers' demographics and the frequency of usage of audios in WhatsApp groups, and the other related to impressions they had after listening to the selected audio. We selected a random sample of 100 audios, 50 with unchecked content and 50 with misinformation content. Each audio was evaluated by 3 different people while each volunteer evaluated 5 different audios.

In total, 25 volunteers participated in the online survey. Starting with the responses to the first set of questions, the volunteers were, on average, 27 years old, 16 of them identified themselves as male and 9 as female. Moreover, the largest group they participated in varied from 25 to 256 members, with an aver-

---

[8] This potential bias of the volunteers is not problem in itself as the main focus of this phase was to raise the general impression that audios with misinformation evoked on the volunteers.

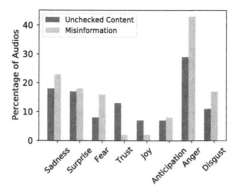

Fig. 2. Emotions felt by listeners of misinformation and unchecked content.

age of 88, which coincides with previous observations that WhatsApp groups tend to connect a large group of people [7,21]. In general, our volunteers reported that they receive audios more often than send them on WhatsApp.

For the second part of the survey, each answer was tied to a specific audio file, and we discuss them separately for audios with misinformation and with unchecked content. First we asked which emotion did the volunteer feel when listened to the audio. Figure 2 shows the percentages of audios for which different emotions were selected by the volunteers when listening to them. For each audio, we considered all the emotions selected by all volunteers. Thus, note that the percentages may exceed 100%. Note that volunteers felt more negative emotions when listening to audio messages with misinformation. This might be due to the higher presence of negative words, as we discussed in Sect. 4.2. Sadness, surprise, fear, disgust, and especially anger were most felt while listening to audios with misinformation, whereas trust and joy were most reported when listening to audios with unchecked content.

When asking whether did they think the audio contained false information, when presented audios with misinformation, our volunteers spotted them 76% of the time. When asked whether the audio had some form of data or source to back the information, 58% responded yes when presented an audio with misinformation and only 17% responded yes when presented an audio with unchecked content. However, when asked whether the provided source increased the credibility of the audio, only 24% of the volunteers said it did indeed increase the credibility. This reaffirms some points raised by the volunteers of the interview: many audios with misinformation try to back their history with some study or data, but they are often not reliable enough. This also links back to the greater prevalence of the *insight* attribute in audios with misinformation, as reported in Sect. 4.2. Words that characterize this attribute, such as "think", "consider", "know", are often used to create a storyline. Overall, most volunteers said they would not share any of the audios with friends or family: indeed, for audios with misinformation, only 9% of the volunteers mentioned that they would share them, whereas, for audios with unchecked content, this fraction drops to 5%.

We then preceded to ask about the naturality, excitement, and friendliness of the audio. Each volunteer was able to select a number from zero to four for each of the three questions. For naturality, zero indicated "Very Artificial" whereas four indicated "Very Natural". As for excitement and friendliness, zero indicated "Very Sad" and "Very Hostile", and four indicated "Very Excited" and "Very Friendly" respectively. We found a significant difference in the answers of volunteers regarding the *naturality* and *friendliness* of the speakers for audios with misinformation and with unchecked content, but no significant difference with respect to *excitement*. Volunteers reported that speakers of audios with misinformation tend to be more often less friendly (average score of 1.78) than speakers of audios with unchecked content (average score of 2.34), with a statistically significant difference according to a t-test (p-value ≤ 0.05). As to the naturality of the speaker, the gap is even larger: the average score was 1.65 for audios with misinformation and 2.56 for unchecked content (statistically significant difference with p-value ≤ 0.05). That is, speakers of audios with misinformation tend to more often give the impression of an artificial tone. Lastly, when asking whether the audio had any call to action, volunteers reported that they could often identify this characteristic in audios with misinformation. Indeed, some type of instruction to be executed by the listener (e.g., *share the audio in more groups*) was reported in 72% of the cases of audios with misinformation. For audios with unchecked content, this fraction falls to 32%.

In sum, the survey results suggest the following key observations. Audios with misinformation tend to make the listeners feel more negative emotions, such as sadness, fear, anger, and disgust, and more often mention some source to try to support their claims, although these sources were often seen as unreliable and, in many cases, did not make the information more believable. Moreover, the speaker's tone of audios with misinformation was considered less *friendly* and less *natural* than the audios with unchecked content. Finally, audios with misinformation more often resorted to some type of call to action, notably as a strategy to help spread the content.

5   Propagation Dynamics

In this section, we look into the propagation dynamics of audio messages, looking into the metrics lifetime and inter-share time. The former is the time interval between the first and the last times a particular audio content was shared in any monitored group, $t_n - t_1$, where n represents the number of times the audio was shared in any group, whereas the latter is the time interval between consecutive shares of the same content (regardless of the group in which it was shared), $t_2 - t_1, ..., t_n - t_{n-1}$. We also look into how many groups each audio message reaches and how many unique users share the same audio.

Figure 3a shows the distributions of lifetimes for audios with misinformation and unchecked content. As shown, audios with misinformation tend to last longer on the platform: 75% of audios with misinformation remained being (re-)shared by up to 31 days, whereas the same fraction of audios with unchecked content

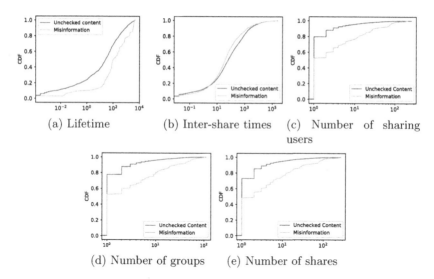

(a) Lifetime

(b) Inter-share times

(c) Number of sharing users

(d) Number of groups

(e) Number of shares

Fig. 3. Propagation dynamics of misinformation and with unchecked audios.

lasted at most 7 days. These numbers represent a significant increase compared to prior results on image messages. According to [22], no significant difference in the lifetimes of images with misinformation and unchecked content was observed, as roughly 70% of images in either category lasted up to 100 h. With respect to textual messages, on the other hand, prior results [21] are somewhat similar to what was observed here for audios, though with longer lifetimes. For instance, 50% of textual messages with misinformation lasted up to 10 days in the system. In contrast, here we observe that the same fraction of audios with misinformation lasts for up to 6 days.

Figure 3b shows the distributions of inter-share times. We see only a small difference in the distributions for misinformation and unchecked content. Roughly speaking, around half of the audios with misinformation are re-shared within 40 min whereas the same fraction of audios with unchecked content are re-shared within 65 min. Thus, audios with misinformation tend to spread slightly more quickly than unchecked ones. This result is consistent with prior findings that misinformation in both image and textual content spreads faster. However, audios with misinformation tend to spread much more quickly than images with misinformation: according to [21], around 80% of the images with misinformation are re-shared within 100 min, but we found that only 65% of the audios with misinformation are re-shared with the same time interval.

We now turn to the analysis of the reach of the audio messages, in terms of number of users who shared them and number of groups where they were shared. Note that the latter gives an idea of the potential audience of these messages. Figure 3c shows that audios with misinformation tend to be shared by a larger number of distinct users: around 80% of audios with misinformation are shared by at least 12 different users, while 80% of unchecked audio are shared by at most two people. Also, as shown in Fig. 3d, audios with misinformation tend to reach a much larger potential audience: 90% of audios with misinformation are shared in at least 27 different groups, while the same fraction of audios with unchecked content appears only in three groups. Ultimately, Fig. 3e shows that audios with misinformation tend to be shared a much larger number of times: 20% of them were shared more than 13 times, while 80% of the audios unchecked content had a maximum share count of only two.

These numbers show the greater potential of "viralization" that audios with misinformation have over general, unchecked audio. Indeed, audios with misinformation tend to often target topics that are incredibly relevant to the political scenario that they appear in, such as political candidates during the electoral period, or involving major opinions toward strikes, as seen in Sect. 4.1. They also bring many psychological attributes that catch people's attention and have a direct impact on our emotions, such as the use of negative words, or attributes regarding future, as seen in Sect. 4.2 and even in the response from the interviews conducted in Sect. 4.3. Finally, they include contents that make them potentially more engaging, such as "sources" that try to back their stories or employ strategies to engage the listener in actions (e.g., re-sharing), as seen in Sect. 4.3. These observed characteristics of audios with misinformation are consistent with prior findings for images and textual messages as well [21,22] and may contribute to their attractiveness and virality. An avenue of future work is to explore the greater presence of these properties in the design of methods to detect misinformation and mitigate its harmful impact.

6   Conclusions and Future Work

Recent studies looked at the propagation of textual and image content in WhatsApp, but to our knowledge, no study focused on misinformation in audio content. In that context, our goal was to understand of how audio messages with misinformation are used in publicly accessible WhatsApp groups. We first focused on understanding the characteristics of these audio messages in terms of content properties and propagation dynamics, while also looking at the differences to prior findings for text and images.

Regarding the topics discussed in the audios, four were directly related to politics and had the largest fraction of misinformation. Other discussion topics were related to religion and chatter. Analyzing the psychological attributes, we identified a higher presence of words related to negative emotions and insight states in audios with misinformation. They also had more phrases in the future tense and referring directly to the listener using pronouns such as "you". Prior analyses on WhatsApp textual content found the frequent presence of terms that aggregate people, such as "we", and verbs often in the present tense. Thus, indicating different types of approaches depending on the type of media used.

We conducted a qualitative analysis to deepen our knowledge about the audio messages, gathering the perception of selected volunteers on the audio's content and potential feelings the speaker's voice triggered, analyzing audios with misinformation and with unchecked content separately. One key result from that analysis is that audios with misinformation tend to more often make the listener feel negative emotions, such as sadness and anger. Also, audios with misinformation often tried to back their claims by citing some sources, often perceived by the volunteers as unreliable. The speaker's tone from the audios with misinformation was considered less *friendly* and less *natural* than audios with unchecked content. Lastly, volunteers also noted that audios with misinformation carried some instruction for the listener, such as sharing the audio with other groups.

Finally, we looked into how these audios propagated in these groups. We observed that misinformation audios appear in more groups, are shared by more users, and have overall more shares than unchecked content. Many factors can explain it, such as being targeted for incredibly relevant topics to the political scenario that they appear in and having attributes that catch people's attention, and directly impacting the listeners' emotions.

A possible direction for the future consists of expanding our analysis to account for audios shared across many years, looking into how these properties behave across time, and possibly detecting seasonal events. We also would like to compare how the messages behave across the same topics of discussion. Lastly, another direction is to expand our misinformation detection pipeline to reliably and automatically detect audios with misinformation, thus expanding our current analysis to a larger quantity of audio files.

References

1. Allcott, H., Gentzkow, M.: Social media and fake news in the 2016 election. J. Econ. Perspect. **31**(2), 211–236 (2017)
2. Baeth, M., Aktas, M.: Detecting misinformation in social networks using provenance data. In: SKG (2017)
3. Bessi, A., Ferrara, E.: Social bots distort the 2016 US presidential election online discussion. First Monday **21**(11–7) (2016)
4. Blei, D., Ng, A., Jordan, M.: Latent Dirichlet allocation. JMLR **3**(Jan), 993–1022 (2003)
5. Broniatowski, D., et al.: Weaponized health communication: Twitter bots and Russian trolls amplify the vaccine debate. Ame. J. Public Health **108**(10), 1378–1384 (2018)
6. Bursztyn, V., Birnbaum, L.: Thousands of small, constant rallies: a large-scale analysis of partisan WhatsApp groups. In: ASONAM 2019 (2019)
7. Caetano, J., Magno, G., Gonçalves, M., Almeida, J., Marques-Neto, H., Almeida, V.: Characterizing attention cascades in WhatsApp groups. In: WebSci 2019 (2019)
8. Cunningham, S., Ridley, H., Weinel, J., Picking, R.: Supervised machine learning for audio emotion recognition. Pers. Ubiquit. Comput. **25**(4), 637–650 (2020). https://doi.org/10.1007/s00779-020-01389-0
9. Fernando, G.: Why people are switching from texting to voice messages (2018). www.news.com.au/technology/gadgets/mobile-phones/why-people-are-switching -from-texting-to-voice-messages/news-story/d36d6d80cc0c71da168b4e8ec96924e7. Accessed 23 Feb 2021
10. Ferrara, E., Varol, O., Davis, C., Menczer, F., Flammini, A.: The rise of social bots. Commun. ACM **59**(7), 96–104 (2016)

11. Garimella, K., Eckles, D.: Images and misinformation in political groups: evidence from WhatsApp in India. HKS Misinform. Rev. (2020)
12. Graves, L.: Deciding what's true: fact-checking journalism and the new ecology of news. Ph.D. thesis, Columbia University (2013)
13. Maros, A., Almeida, J., Benevenuto, F., Vasconcelos, M.: Analyzing the use of audio messages in whatsapp groups. In: TheWebConf (2020)
14. Melo, P., Messias, J., Resende, G., Garimella, K., Almeida, J., Benevenuto, F.: WhatsApp monitor: a fact-checking system for WhatsApp. In: ICWSM 2019 (2019)
15. Melo, P., Vieira, C., Garimella, K., Melo, P., Benevenuto, F.: Can WhatsApp counter misinformation by limiting message forwarding? In: ICCA 2019 (2019)
16. Menczer, F.: The spread of misinformation in social media. In: TheWebConf (2016)
17. Moon, A., Raju, T.: A survey on document clustering with similarity measures. IJERT **3**(11), 599–601 (2013)
18. Nobre, G.P., Ferreira, C.H.G., Almeida, J.M.: Beyond groups: uncovering dynamic communities on the WhatsApp network of information dissemination. In: Aref, S., et al. (eds.) SocInfo 2020. LNCS, vol. 12467, pp. 252–266. Springer, Cham (2020). https://doi.org/10.1007/978-3-030-60975-7_19
19. Pennebaker, J., Boyd, R., Jordan, K., Blackburn, K.: The development and psychometric properties of liwc2015. Technical report (2015)
20. Reis, J., Melo, P., Garimella, K., Benevenuto, F.: Can whatsapp benefit from debunked fact-checked stories to reduce misinformation? (2020)
21. Resende, G., Melo, P., Reis, J., Vasconcelos, M., Almeida, J., Benevenuto, F.: Analyzing textual (mis)information shared in WhatsApp groups. In: WebSci (2019)
22. Resende, G., et al.: (mis)information dissemination in WhatsApp: gathering, analyzing and countermeasures. In: TheWebConf (2019)
23. Sherman, L., Michikyan, M., Greenfield, P.: The effects of text, audio, video, and in-person communication on bonding between friends. Cyberpsychology **7**(2) (2013)

Hide and Seek in Slovakia: Utilizing Tracking Code Data to Uncover Untrustworthy Website Networks

Jozef Michal Mintal[1,2(✉)] ⓘ, Michal Kalman[3], and Karol Fabián[1] ⓘ

[1] Department of Security Studies and UMB Data & Society Lab at CEKR, Matej Bel University, Banská Bystrica, Slovakia
jozef.mintal@umb.sk
[2] Center for Media, Data and Society at CEU Democracy Institute, Central European University, Budapest, Hungary
[3] Morione, Bratislava, Slovakia

Abstract. The proliferation of misleading or false information spread by untrustworthy websites has emerged as a significant concern on the public agenda in many countries, including Slovakia. Despite the influence ascribed to such websites, their transparency and accountability remain an issue in most cases, with published work on mapping the administrators and connections of untrustworthy websites remaining limited. This article contributes to this body of knowledge (i) by providing an effective open-source tool to uncover untrustworthy website networks based on the utilization of the same Google Analytics/AdSense IDs, with the added ability to expose networks based on historical data, and (ii) by providing insight into the Slovak untrustworthy website landscape through delivering a first of its kind mapping of Slovak untrustworthy website networks. Our approach is based on a mix-method design employing a qualitative exploration of data collected in a two-wave study conducted in 2019 and 2021, utilizing a custom-coded tool to uncover website connections. Overall, the study succeeds in exposing multiple novel website ties. Our findings indicate that while some untrustworthy website networks have been found to operate in the Slovak infosphere, most researched websites appear to be run by multiple mutually unconnected administrators. The resulting data also demonstrates that untrustworthy Slovak websites display a high content diversity in terms of connected websites, ranging from websites of local NGOs, an e-shop selling underwear to a matchmaking portal.

Keywords: Untrustworthy websites · Wayback machine · Slovakia · Google analytics · AdSense · Website networks

1 Introduction

The burgeoning of misleading or false information in cyberspace has emerged as a central concern on the public agenda in recent years [1], fueled by, among other things, the sprouting of untrustworthy websites across many countries around the world, with Slovakia being no exception [2]. Notwithstanding that these untrustworthy websites [3],

J. Bright et al. (Eds.): MISDOOM 2021, LNCS 12887, pp. 101–111, 2021.
https://doi.org/10.1007/978-3-030-87031-7_7

in some instances, have been ascribed to exercise far-reaching influence over the public discourse [1, 4], transparency and accountability of such websites remain an issue in most cases [5], with multiple websites remaining shrouded in anonymity. A useful approach that has crystallized in data journalism to uncover connections among websites and map untrustworthy website networks [6], has been a technique utilizing third-party tracking IDs mainly used by web analytics and ad serving services.

Web analytics is an indispensable tool for any website to understand and optimize its web usage [7], with a significant number of website administrators opting for a freemium third-party service such as Google Analytics [8]. Given that the client sides of such third-party services report to the same centralized backend, the client requests need to contain distinctive identifiers for the backend servers to differentiate between clients. However, such a setup is not exclusive to technologies tracking web usage but is also present in various other third-party services, such as the widely utilized ad serving service AdSense. The utilization of these third-party services among Slovak and Czech untrustworthy websites is high, with the most popular analytics technology being Google Analytics [9]. For convenience and in some cases also per the services' applicable terms and conditions [10], website administrators often manage their websites under a single identifier (ID). As a side result of using a single ID across multiple websites, it is possible to uncover connections between domains that otherwise seem unconnected. As this tracking code technique has garnered wider attention, it is possible that website administrators might have dissociated their IDs across their websites, which in return poses threats to the current widely utilized approaches aimed at uncovering such networks.

Notwithstanding that the threat posed by untrustworthy websites is a central concern on the public agenda [1], published work on untrustworthy website network detection remains limited, with work on this topic largely confined to reports and articles by non-governmental organizations, enthusiastic code developers and investigative journalists [11, 12]. As for the work exploring untrustworthy website networks in Slovakia, the inquiry remains even more so limited, with only a few investigative reporting pieces by local journalists [13, 14]. Thus, the aim of this paper is two-fold, (i) to provide an effective open-source tool to uncover untrustworthy website networks utilizing the same Google Analytics and AdSense IDs, with the added ability to expose networks based on historically associated IDs; and (ii) to provide insight into the Slovak untrustworthy website landscape by delivering a first of its kind mapping of Slovak untrustworthy website networks. To achieve the above aim, the presented article first offers a short state of the filed overview as well as background information on the untrustworthy websites landscape in Slovakia. Then, it introduces the methods and results of our empirical study, utilizing a highly effective custom python script used to uncover website connections in a longitudinal study of untrustworthy Slovak websites, with data collection undertaken first in April/May 2019 and then in April/May 2021. In the results section of this article, we then also present a short qualitative description of two untrustworthy Slovak website networks. Finally, based on the findings of our study, at the end of this article, we provide a brief discussion highlighting limitations as well as charting possible avenues for future research.

1.1 Related Work

The utilization of website tracking codes to uncover hidden connections between websites was likely first reported by Baio in 2011 [15]. However, the technique garnered wider attention in the disinformation research community mostly after a social media analyst named Lawrence Alexander published in 2015 an investigative report in which he utilized Google Analytics IDs to uncover a pro-Kremlin web campaign [11]. However, the published approach was laborious and hardly scalable as it heavily relied on a manual component. This laboriousness prompted Seitz and Alexander to release a computer script in 2015 [16], which automated some of the tasks. The script was in 2017 updated as a number of the backend services it relied upon closed down [17]. It is around this time that also some academic scholarship on this topic emerged [7]. The utilization of Google Analytics and Google AdSense IDs to uncover untrustworthy website networks has become nowadays a staple in data journalism, however, with journalists still oftentimes relying on manual data collection [6]. As the tracking code linking technique has become better know also among the wider public, it might be argued that untrustworthy website administrators might have taken steps to dissociate their Analytics and AdSense IDs across their websites, which in return poses threats to the current publicly available scripts aimed at uncovering such networks [17]. As for the work exploring untrustworthy website networks in Slovakia, the inquiry remains scarce, confined mainly to a couple of traditional qualitatively based investigative journalism pieces, notably by Benčík [18] and Šnídl [19], and investigative data journalism pieces notably by Breiner [13, 14]. With the latter one mentioned succeeding in uncovering two higher-profile untrustworthy website networks, both spreading predominantly false health claims [13, 14].

1.2 The Slovak Untrustworthy Website Landscape

Untrustworthy websites have in recent years started to burgeon across many countries around the world, with Slovakia being no exception to this practice. However, the exact number of such websites, including in Slovakia, is difficult to pinpoint. This situation is, among other things, fueled by the fact that websites can, in general, get easily taken down or redirected to a different domain, while new websites can, due to relatively low entrance barriers, be created also reasonably quickly [2]. As for the Slovak untrustworthy websites landscape, the most comprehensive publicly available list of such websites is compiled by a local media watchdog named Konšpirátori.sk [20]. The list, which is heavily relied upon by local researchers and policy experts [2, 21], ranks websites on a ten-point scale. Those scoring more than six points are considered to have highly dubious, deceptive, fraudulent, conspiratorial or propaganda content [22]. As of the end of May 2021, konspiratori.sk lists 210 websites with a score higher than six [20]. Thematically the websites tracked in the konspiratori.sk list cover a wide range of topics, including, among others, health disinformation, Russian propaganda, and the paranormal. According to website traffic data estimates by SimilarWeb, some of the Slovak untrustworthy websites boast a high number of monthly visitors, with some of these websites even ranking in the top 100 most visited websites in Slovakia [2, 9]. However, transparency remains an issue in most of the cases. Multiple websites were shown to be actively trying to conceal their identity by, among other things, utilizing various domain privacy services or offshore hosting [5]. From a financial perspective, untrustworthy Slovak websites rely on various business models to sustain operation, with popular income sources including tax designation, e-commerce, crowdfunding, and advertising [5].

2 Methods

To study the networks of untrustworthy Slovak websites, we used a mix-method approached employing a qualitative exploration of data collected from a custom coded python script tasked to uncover websites using the same Google Analytics/AdSense identifier. The research was approved by the Matej Bel University (UMB) Ethics Committee (Reference no.: 1113-2017-FF). All methods were performed in accordance with UMB ethics guidance and regulations. Data Collection was conducted in two waves, first in April/May 2019 and then in April/May 2021. For the April/May 2019 data collection phase, our initial untrustworthy websites list consisted of 144 websites, available at that time, taken from the konspiratori.sk database. For the April/May 2021 data collection phase, our initial untrustworthy websites list consisted of 205 websites, also taken from the konspiratori.sk database [20]. Inclusion of a website in the database is based on a set of publicly available criteria, against which a Review Board consisting of, inter alia, prominent historians, political scientists, medical professionals, journalists and civil society representatives assess a website [23]. In utilizing the konspiratori.sk database, we followed best practices used in Slovak disinformation scholarship [2, 5, 21]. Second, each website in our dataset was during the respective data collection phases manually checked to determine its availability status and primary language. Unavailable websites and websites with a primary language other than Slovak were discarded. For the data collection phases, we build a python script, coded in python 2.7.10. The script builds upon code by Alexander and Seitz [16] and Seitz [17]. However, as opposed to their script, our script is based on a modified data collection setup designed to mitigate irrelevant data ballast and filter out data relics from third-party services that it utilizes, such as the Spy on Web API. In addition, our script also incorporates various novel features, most notably a history function, i.e., the ability to collect tracking codes from historical versions of websites, thus helping to evade possible measures undertaken by website administrators to dissociate their Google Analytics and AdSense IDs. For a simplified flowchart of the script, see Fig. 1.

The script underwent multiple rounds of testing and validation, including against manually collected data. The first phase of data collection using our custom python script was carried out during April/May 2019. After downloading the data, the script automatically linked websites based on the utilization of the same Google Analytics/AdSense identifier and created a graph file. Concurrently with the automatic data collection utilizing our script, we also performed a manual data collection, downloading the necessary data about all websites on our untrustworthy website list. The manually collected data represented a validation dataset against which the python-script-based data was compared. The second phase of data collection was carried out in two separate streams during April/May 2021. The first stream aimed to validate the history function of our script, i.e., the ability to collect tracking codes from historical versions of a website. The second stream represented a longitudinal continuation of the first data collection phase conducted in April/May 2019.

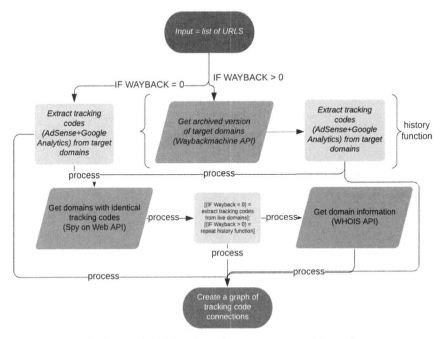

Fig. 1. Simplified flowchart of our custom unmasking script.

After each data collection phase ended, all datasets underwent data cleansing to detect and correct corrupt or inaccurate records. Subsequently, we calculated basic descriptive statistics for the cleansed datasets and identified the most salient disinformation networks. The resulting data from the two data collection phases were then content-coded and qualitatively examined, focusing mainly on the success rate of our approach in uncovering untrustworthy website networks. Last, we formatted the resultant datasets and visualized the data.

3   Results

Out of our initial sample size of 144 untrustworthy websites in the first data collection phase undertaken in April/May 2019, 21 websites appeared to cease to exist, and 74 were found to be primarily in languages other than Slovak, and therefore were discarded from our dataset. In addition, we also discarded three micro-blogging websites, as tracking codes present on such websites are managed by the respective platform operator, e.g., livejournal.com. Thus, our final list of untrustworthy websites for the first data collection phase consisted of 46 entries. As for the second data collection phase, out of our initial sample size of 205 untrustworthy websites, 51 appeared to cease to exist, and 87 were found to be primarily in languages other than Slovak and were therefore discarded from our dataset. In addition, two micro-blogging websites were discarded. Thus, our final list of untrustworthy websites for the second data collection phase consisted of 65 entries. A manual content-coding of the final lists of untrustworthy websites, utilizing a modified framework [9] based on the one developed by Mintal and Rusnak [5], showed that the majority of websites under investigation were in both data collection phases News-Focused; for a more detailed breakdown per each content category see Table 1.

Table 1. Frequency table of websites according to their content category.

Content category	Frequency (April/May 2019 data)	Frequency (April/May 2021 data)
News-Focused	20	39
Ideological or Supporting Cause	9	13
Health and Lifestyle	13	12
Paranormal	4	1

After extensive code review, syntax check and debugging, our custom python script demonstrated a data retrieval accuracy of $= 100.00\%$, validated against four rounds of manually collected data from 20 randomly selected websites. Testing was conducted from December 2018 to February 2019. In addition, the data for all 46 untrustworthy websites on our list was concurrent with the automated data collection utilizing our script, also collected manually. A comparison between the automated and manually collected datasets, with the later one used as a validation dataset, revealed a data retrieval accuracy of $= 100\%$.

The data collected using the script during the April/May 2019 data collection phase showed that 84.79% of websites under investigation contained either a Google Analytics or Google AdSense tracking ID. Out of the 46 websites on our list, 14 websites were uncovered to belong to a network of linked websites, with such ecologies amounting to $(n = 11)$. The largest number of uncovered networks $(n = 6)$ were connected to News-related content-coded untrustworthy websites, $(n = 3)$ were connected to Health and Lifestyle websites, and $(n = 2)$ were connected to Ideological or supporting cause websites. The obtained data about the uncovered networks were during July/August 2019 qualitatively benchmarked against publicly available investigative pieces and data from the Business of Misinformation Project at CEU. The project employed a predominantly qualitative approach to uncover untrustworthy website ownership data in Slovakia, relying on investigative reports, the Investigative Dashboard Databases, self-reported data, and WHOIS data [5]. The benchmarking exercise yielded positive results, with our quantitative approach uncovering ten at that time unknown networks, with some of them internally classified as high-interest ones (e.g., pub-2531845767488846/UA-12857229; pub-9657897336906985; UA-1374898). The classification was based on external and internal consultations with relevant stakeholders. A qualitative analysis of the 12 uncovered networks showed a high diversity of linked websites in these networks, with websites belonging to a local NGO (e.g., UA-5743998), an e-shop selling underwear (UA-1374898), a matchmaking portal (pub-4883385023448719), but in some cases also to multiple other untrustworthy websites spreading dubious health claims (pub-9657897336906985). The descriptive statistics for the uncovered networks for both data collection phases are shown in Table 2.

For the second phase of data collection, set during April/May 2021, the script passed repeated code review and testing. The history function of the script, i.e., the ability to collected tracking codes from historical versions of a website, was validated against data collected in 2019, with a data retrieval accuracy of = 100%. The data collected using the script during the second data collection phase revealed that 67.69% of websites under investigation contained either a Google Analytics or Google AdSense tracking ID. Out of the 65 websites on our untrustworthy website list, 12 websites were identified to belong to a network of connected websites, with such ecologies amounting to (n = 11). The largest number of uncovered networks (n = 7) were linked to News-related content-coded untrustworthy websites from our list, (n = 2) were linked to Health and Lifestyle websites, and (n = 2) were linked to Ideological or supporting cause websites. A qualitative analysis of the 11 uncovered networks again showed a high diversity of affiliated websites in these networks. Compared to the previously identified networks, one network appeared to cease to exist, and a new one was detected (UA-24461628). The descriptive statistics for the uncovered networks for both data collection phases are shown in Table 2.

Table 2. Descriptive statistics for uncovered networks.

	Dimension of networks (n = 11)	Dimension of networks (n = 11)
	(April/May 2019 data)	(April/May 2021 data)
Min—Max	2—9	2—7
Mean	3.636	3.181
SD	1.919	1.465

When exploring the degree of change among the two datasets (2019 and 2021) in terms of websites modifying their Google Analytics ID, Google AdSense ID, or both — out of 46 websites tracked in the first data collection phase, one website has deleted its AdSense ID, one its Google Analytics ID, while three websites have added an additional ID type to their already used one. Comparing the degree of change for the uncovered linked websites is, however, higher, with multiple instances of websites deleting the IDs that connected them to one of the 46 websites on the konspiratori.sk list, with examples including the official website of a high-profile Slovak actor (UA-12857229), or a website of a high-profile Slovak singer (UA-1374898).

3.1 Sample Description of Two Uncovered Networks

As for a qualitative exploration of some of the uncovered networks, considering the nature and page limitations of this short study, we offer a brief case description of two thematically different networks, with the second one being publicized for the first time.

The first network concentrates around AdSense ID — pub-9657897336906985. The network comprises multiple untrustworthy websites spreading dubious health claims, with the network and its perpetrator being publicly disclosed in national media by a local data journalist in 2020 [13]. Breiner's discovery of the existence of such a network was undertaken independently from our 2019 findings, as the data from our first data collection wave were only disclosed on a need-to-know basis to certain stakeholders due to the nature of the information. However, contrary to our research, Breiner's investigative journalism piece also focused on uncovering the identity of the perpetrator — a young man from southern Slovakia [13], who appeared to be running the website network purely due to profit-making. These findings underscore the strong business-focused motives of some perpetrators operating untrustworthy websites. Such motives have also been highlighted by earlier research findings from the Business of misinformation project at CEU, which uncovered that 38 out of 49 researched untrustworthy Slovak websites operating in 2019 displayed ads or sold goods and services [5].

The second network, a previously unpublished one — pub-2531845767488846/UA-12857229 seems to be concentrated around a local IT services company, with a member of the company management shown in the past to directly back the establishment of a now-notorious untrustworthy website named panobcan.sk [24]. The network concentered around panobcan.sk' AdSense/Analytics ID is mainly interesting as in the past it used to be among others connected to a website of a high-profile Slovak actor, or that of *Slovenské národné noviny,* a newspaper officially published by *Matica slovenská* — a Slovak government-funded cultural and scientific institution primarily tasked with cultivating and presenting Slovak national cultural heritage [25]. While it is possible that the linkages among the observed websites stemmed from purely business-oriented grounds, as the company at the center of the website network focuses on providing IT services, at least in the case of the *Slovenské národné noviny,* a connection also appears to be on the content side, with researchers observing various dubious and at times also pro-Kremlin narratives spread in the past by the publisher of the newspaper — *Matica Slovenská* [26].

However, it should be noted that the presented motives or thematic narratives of the two described networks are in no way exhaustive, as the two networks were chosen based on internal and external consultations labelling them as high-interest ones. A narrative analysis of untrustworthy Slovak website networks would, however, represent an interesting avenue for future research.

4   Discussion

The results described above indicate a high data retrieval accuracy, precision, and efficiency of our script in uncovering untrustworthy Slovak website networks. The Slovak data obtained using our script show that while some untrustworthy website networks have been found to operate in the Slovak infosphere, most untrustworthy websites appear to be run by multiple mutually unconnected administrators. However, our data has also demonstrated that untrustworthy Slovak websites display a high content diversity of connected websites, ranging from websites of local NGOs to a matchmaking portal.

Our findings run somewhat counter to popular discourse and published investigations from other countries, in which large-scale foreign influence operations utilizing vast untrustworthy website networks administered from abroad have been discovered [27]. Our data on untrustworthy Slovak website networks rather indicates that they are largely domestically based.

However, the inhere presented approach of uncovering untrustworthy website networks is certainly not without limitations, which stem mainly from four interlinked sources. First, even though the utilization rate of Google Analytics and AdSense IDs is generally high, especially among the inhere researched Slovak websites, not all untrustworthy websites use these services. Second, it has to be noted that while the usage of the same ID across multiple websites administered by the same publisher is highly convenient and, in the case of AdSense, also mandated as per the services' Terms and conditions [10], publishers can still theoretically find ways to circumvent this requirement. However, such bypassing would require ample resources, as AdSense technically prohibits accounts with duplicate payee records, which get verified using the user's bank details, and in some countries also via an SMS code, or a physically mailed out PIN code. The third source of limitation is more of a technical nature as due to the vast and dynamically growing number of websites in existence, it cannot be ruled out that not all websites with the same ID have been yet indexed or recently crawled by the third-party services that our script relies on. However, owing to the setup of the utilized services, it is likely that such possibly occurring websites are assumably either very recently established, lower traffic or both. The fourth source of limitation of this study stems from the fact that some untrustworthy websites might potentially be connected through financially or otherwise related parties outside of the digital realm, such as relatives, business partners, shell companies, and others. Hence, although the benchmarking exercise of our approach indicates high precision and efficiency in uncovering untrustworthy Slovak website networks, this does not mean that our approach is able to uncover all connections of untrustworthy websites. Steaming from the discussed limitations and our results, we consider several avenues for future work. First, given among others, the possible differences in utilization rates of Google Analytics and AdSense across different websites leaves room for future work on modifying our script to extend its functionality and be able to link websites also based on other types of tracking IDs. Moreover, as other untrustworthy networks get discovered in the future, the collected data opens up, among others, possibilities for better understanding the motives and behaviour of the perpetrators administering such websites.

In conclusion, besides providing an effective open-source tool to uncover untrustworthy website networks, with the added ability to expose networks based on historical data, our article also delivered a first of its kind mapping of untrustworthy Slovak website networks, showing among others that untrustworthy Slovak websites appear to be run by multiple mutually unconnected administrators. Overall, we hope that our open-source script and this study's results will assist not only various actors combating online disinformation but also encourage further work on uncovering and understanding untrustworthy website networks and the possible ways of addressing issues related to this vital topic.

Funding and Declaration of Conflicting Interest. This work was supported by IBM (IBM Faculty Award 2017), VEGA (grant project n. 1/0433/18) and APVV (grant project n. APVV-20-0334). The authors declared no potential conflicts of interest with respect to the research, authorship, and/or publication of this article.

Contributions. J.M.M. designed the study; M.K. coded the python script with input from J.M.M.; K.F. supervised the research and provided funding; J.M.M. collected the data and analyzed the data with input from K.F.; J.M.M. wrote the paper with input from K.F. All authors reviewed the results and approved the final version of the manuscript.

Data Availability. The code is available via GitHub at https://doi.org/10.5281/zenodo.4783300; the code is published under a GNU General Public License. The data that support the findings of this study have been deposited in Zenodo at https://doi.org/10.5281/zenodo.4783287; the data are available upon reasonable request.

References

1. Tenove, C.: Protecting democracy from disinformation: normative threats and policy responses. Int. J. Press/Polit. **25**, 517–537 (2020). https://doi.org/10.1177/1940161220918740
2. Klingova, K.: What Do We Know About Disinformation Websites in the Czech Republic and Slovakia? https://www.globsec.org/news/what-do-we-know-about-disinformation-websites-in-the-czech-republic-and-slovakia/. Accessed 23 March 2021
3. Guess, A.M., Nyhan, B., Reifler, J.: Exposure to untrustworthy websites in the 2016 US election. Nat. Hum. Behav. **4**, 472–480 (2020). https://doi.org/10.1038/s41562-020-0833-x
4. Ognyanova, K., Lazer, D., Robertson, R.E., Wilson, C.: Misinformation in action: fake news exposure is linked to lower trust in media, higher trust in government when your side is in power. HKS Misinfo Review (2020). https://doi.org/10.37016/mr-2020-024
5. Mintal, J.M.: Slovakia: snake oil spills onto the web. In: The Unbearable Ease of Misinformation. Center for Media, Data and Society at Central European University, Budapest (2020)
6. Rogers, R.: Doing Digital Methods. SAGE Publications, Thousand Oaks, CA (2019)
7. Starov, O., Zhou, Y., Zhang, X., Miramirkhani, N., Nikiforakis, N.: Betrayed by your dashboard: discovering malicious campaigns via web analytics. In: Proceedings of the 2018 World Wide Web Conference on World Wide Web - WWW 2018. pp. 227–236. ACM Press, Lyon, France (2018). https://doi.org/10.1145/3178876.3186089
8. Google Analytics Usage Statistics. https://web.archive.org/web/20210505184458/https://trends.builtwith.com/analytics/Google-Analytics. Accessed 27 May 2021
9. Mintal, J.M., et al.: Examining the tech stacks of Czech and Slovak untrustworthy websites. In: ICOMTA (2021)
10. Google AdSense - Terms and Conditions (2021). https://www.google.com/adsense/new/localized-terms?hl=en_US
11. Alexander, L.: Open-Source Information Reveals Pro-Kremlin Web Campaign Global Voices. https://globalvoices.org/2015/07/13/open-source-information-reveals-pro-kremlin-web-campaign/. Accessed 23 May 2021

12. How Google Analytics Codes Unearthed a Network of South African Fake News Sites. https://www.bellingcat.com/news/africa/2017/08/04/guptaleaks-google-analytics/. Accessed 23 May 2021
13. Breiner, V.: Pán Báječný: Zásah webov zdieľajúcich propagandu ĽSNS sa ráta už v státisícoch. https://www.aktuality.sk/clanok/758933/konspiracie-fake-news-polacky-propaganda-lsns-volby-2020/. Accessed 20 May 2021
14. Breiner, V.: Digitálne vyšetrovanie: anonymná konšpiračná Facebooková stránka IdemVoliť.sk je prepojená na lekára z Považskej Bystrice. https://infosecurity.sk/domace/idemvolit-sk/. Accessed 23 May 2021
15. Baio, A.: Think You Can Hide, Anonymous Blogger? Two Words: Google Analytics I WIRED. https://www.wired.com/2011/11/goog-analytics-anony-bloggers/. Accessed 02 June 2021
16. Seitz, J., Alexander, L.: Automatically Discover Website Connections Through Tracking Codes (2015)
17. Seitz, J.: website_connections.py. https://github.com/automatingosint/osint_public. Accessed 18 May 2021
18. Benčík, J.: Norbert Lichtner – suverén či suterén Slobodného vysielača? https://dennikn.sk/blog/66617/norbert-lichtner-suveren-ci-suteren-slobodneho-vysielaca/. Accessed 04 June 2021
19. Šnídl, V.: Kto zarába na hoaxoch o rakovine: obchodník z Prešova, ktorý predáva výživové doplnky za 50 eur – Denník N. https://dennikn.sk/1008402/kto-zaraba-na-hoaxoch-o-rakovine-obchodnik-z-presova-ktory-predava-vyzivove-doplnky-za-50-eur/. Accessed 24 May 2021
20. Konspiratori.sk: List of websites with controversial content. https://www.konspiratori.sk/. Accessed 23 March 2021
21. Šimalčík, M.: Image of China in Slovakia: ambivalence, adoration, and fake news. Asia. Eur. J. **19**(2), 245–258 (2021). https://doi.org/10.1007/s10308-021-00597-4
22. Konspiratori.sk - public database of websites with dubious, deceptive, fraudulent or propaganda content. https://www.konspiratori.sk/en. Accessed 22 May 2021
23. Konspiratori.sk: Criteria for including a website in the database. https://www.konspiratori.sk/en/inclusion-criteria.php. Accessed 26 March 2021
24. Panobcan.sk I Ing. Peter Divéky. https://web.archive.org/web/20210301230242/http://peterdiveky.sk/panobcan-sk/. Accessed 04 June 2021
25. 68/1997 Coll. Laws — Law from February 13, 1997 on the "Matica slovenská" (1997)
26. Golianová, V., Kazharski, A.: 'The unsolid': pro-kremlin narratives in Slovak cultural and educational institutions. RUSI J. **165**, 10–21 (2020). https://doi.org/10.1080/03071847.2020.1796521
27. Influencing Policymakers with Fake Media Outlets: An Investigation In to A Pro-Indian Influence Network. EU Disinfo Lab (2019)

The German Comment Landscape

A Structured Overview of the Opportunities for Participatory Discourse on News Websites

Marco Niemann[(✉)] [iD], Kilian Müller [iD], Chantal Kelm, Dennis Assenmacher [iD], and Jörg Becker [iD]

Department for Information Systems, University of Münster,
Leonardo-Campus 3, 48149 Münster, Germany
marco.niemann@ercis.uni-muenster.de

Abstract. Online comment sections revolutionised the participatory discourse as enabled by news media, limiting the hurdles to participate and speeding up the process from submission to publication. What was initially meant to strengthen public debates and democracy turned out to suffer from abusive use: Be it insulting journalists, posting misinformation, or pure hate. While many publishers and journalists are eager to create an engaged audience, user-generated content typically does not create direct revenues. However, keeping the abuse at bay is often obligatory from an ethical and legal perspective and can be costly. Germany has been highly affected by abuse in combination with strict regulation, leading to the shutdown of many comment sections. While reports in 2014 indicated closure rates of 50% and more, a structured overview of the situation in 2020/21 is missing. We conducted a structured assessment of 114 German newspaper websites containing all major outlets to account for this. Our analyses indicate that the deteriorating trend regarding the availability of comment sections slowed down in Germany. However, there are still open issues such as a high number of outlets using post-moderation and limited audience participation options. This provides a reference to researchers and practitioners working on (semi-) automated moderation systems regarding the expectable market and problem size.

Keywords: Web content analysis · Comment sections · Newspapers · Structured overview.

1 Introduction

For a long time, one of the central roles of journalists and journalism has been the so-called gatekeeping: Filtering events, information, and options that are deemed relevant for the audience [4]. Beyond the distribution of factual information and journalistic opinion pieces, the facilitation of public discourse and debate have been part of the journalistic self-understanding as well [20,32]. Traditionally, letters to the editor have been one of the approaches to allow for reader feedback,

© Springer Nature Switzerland AG 2021
J. Bright et al. (Eds.): MISDOOM 2021, LNCS 12887, pp. 112–127, 2021.
https://doi.org/10.1007/978-3-030-87031-7_8

still leaving the journalists and editors far-reaching gatekeeping options [34]. Beyond this, letters to the editor are inherently biased to a small subset of the overall population—predominantly educated, white, middle-aged men [11].

With the advent of the internet and linked technologies the means became available that allowed to broaden the range of participants [5, 26, 28]. Furthermore, the journalist's gatekeeping role was limited by these new technologies [1], as content generated by readers was increasingly published in almost real-time in direct proximity to the article being commented [1]. Even though the share of actively participating readers is still low, research shows that people are taking up these given opportunities to share their opinions—with both journalists and fellow readers [28]. In numbers, this means, for example, in Germany, only less than 25% of the readers regularly contribute comments, but 42% read these actively, indicating a considerable audience [48]. Despite other forms of interactivity being available, commenting is the key feature aimed at participation and expression that is subjected to discourse [25]—and will hence also be at the core of the study at hand.

For newspapers and publishers, comment sections and other forms of participatory journalism have been a complex topic right from the beginning. While early on, many understood that increased reader engagement might be the key to ongoing economic success, limitations such as legal and organisational problems were on decision makers' minds too [1, 38]. One of the core problems soon turned out to be what is nowadays subsumed under terms such as "incivility" or "abusive language"—a trend that has been observed by journalists [2, 18] and academics alike [10, 29]. Some even phrased this as a constant decline from a promising concept to a necessary evil [25], whereas more radical voices even proclaim a complete failure of comment sections (for such voices cf., [23]).

To counter incivility—and this is required from newspapers, be it due to legal obligations or fears of scaring away their audience—newspapers are left with basically two ample choices: invest into moderation and community management to keep incivility at bay or to get rid of their comment sections [23]. Especially the investment into moderation and community management is often significant because commenting is free of charge. However, increasing reviewing quantities takes up considerable amounts of journalists' time [25]. As a consequence, an increasing number of newspapers is deciding against moderated on-site comment sections [15]—reaching up to 50% of newspapers in Germany reporting the cancellation of their comment sections [40].

However, many of the reports available—as indicated above—are already 3–5 years old. Furthermore, many are anecdotal reports [15] or based on surveys with only limited response rates [40]. Academics such as [1] also point out that many of the studies conducted in the overall area are strictly qualitative. This is problematic, as a growing stream of research sets forth to tackle this issue with machine learning-based systems [16, 33]—however, it is unclear how large the problem is and how big of a potential customer base they might expect. Therefore, an up-to-date, structured, quantitative overview of available comment sections is needed in order to assess the impact on newspapers and their users.

As Germany is one of the countries that is caught in a conflict between ensuring free speech but having strict restrictions on illegal speech [14] and exhibiting one of the highest closure rates of comment sections, it makes for an interesting case for an assessment of the status quo. Hence, the research goal of our work is to *create a structured overview of the German commentscape in online newspapers, outlining the existing opportunities for participatory discourse.*

The remainder of this work is structured as follows: Sect. 2 provides an overview of central concepts discussed throughout the paper. In Sect. 3, we explain the sampling procedure for the analysed newspapers and the analytical process itself. The results are outlined in Sect. 4, before the paper is closed off by the discussion in Sect. 5 and the limitations in Sect. 6.

2   Research Background

2.1   Audience Pariticipation in Digital Newspapers

Historically, the term "newspaper" refers to a printed product distributed as a physical copy "broadcasting" news to an audience. The audience itself had few options for participation—typically, at most, the letters to the editor. Through digitalisation and interactive media such as the internet, this classical role distribution changed. The inhibition threshold for communication has fallen noticeably in recent years [8]. First with the introduction of e-mails (digitising the letter to the editor) and followed by the technical possibilities to include user-generated content directly on websites [19]. This content is usually created by the user in a guided/fixed form (e.g., surveys) or can be freely edited (e.g., comments, pictures, URLs). Furthermore, comment sections offer opportunities to reply to or rate other users' comments, enabling direct interaction between the readers. To allow users to generate content, they have to interact with the presented articles or advertisements. Technically, many newspapers realise this through proprietary, individual solutions or the embedding of third-party software; so-called plug-ins [9]. Apart from comment sections, users can leave comments on the newspapers' social media representations (e.g., Facebook, Twitter, YouTube, and Instagram) [22]. From the newspaper's perspective, the developments in participation opportunities for readers are positive, as comments can draw attention to errors, provide pointers for further reporting, and clarifications for other readers. User-generated content can thus be used in various work steps for the creation of the articles. In addition, by sharing the articles via social media, there is a chance that readers also forward these to their friends and families, resulting in a wider reach and awareness, which is an important part of their business model [27].

On the contrary, the additional participation opportunities pose new challenges to newspapers. If the user-generated content contains abusive language or hate speech, it might represent a criminal offense, and the outlets must react. Therefore, newspapers have explored different opportunities to create hurdles for posting user comments. With the knowledge that there are topics that elicit certain reactions in readers [10,24], some newspapers decided not to open up the comment sections for such articles at all (e.g., on the subject of the refugee crisis or court rulings) [4,17]. However, as this approach also hinders democratic discourse, additional approaches can be considered to contain the publication of critical comments. Countering the online disinhibition effect [3], the anonymity of users can be weakened or completely lifted. Towards this end, newspapers have introduced participatory hurdles for the reader. Commenting without a hurdle means commenting anonymously without any form of registration. Thus, the first hurdle is only to allow users to comment if they are registered on the respective website—still using a nickname. Next, users can be forced to register with their real identity, linking their comments to their offline persona. As a further step, users can be forced to comment via their social media profiles. Another possibility is only to allow those users to write comments which have already purchased the newspaper, introducing a monetary hurdle. However, even the addition of multiple hurdles does not guarantee a clean and constructive discourse. Therefore, newspapers can also use pre- and post-moderation efforts in order to reduce the number of critical comments [37]. In case of pre-moderation, the written comment is not immediately publicly visible. Instead, it is forwarded to the journalists or community managers, checked, and then released if it does not violate any law or community guidelines, thus preventing the publication of illegal content [24]. In this way, quality assurance of the content occurs, and the newspaper retains control over its comment sections. By utilising post-moderation, content is first published and later reviewed [36]. The advantage of this type of moderation is that not every comment has to be reviewed, but only those that have been classified as problematic by other readers [35] or those that are found through a review of the comment sections.

2.2   Previous Research on the State of Participatory Options

Currently a structured review of how many newspapers offer comment sections, employ which types of moderation, and introduce which types of hurdles to ensure their comment section remains as constructive as possible is missing in literature. Most scientific sources analyse the content of comments itself, or the influence of different factors on user comments' generation [8,10,39]. However, few scientific sources analyse the general comment landscape, forms of participation, and moderation forms. Domingo et al. [13] explore participation forms in 16 western newspapers to identify the formats of user-generated content published on the websites. These include, among others, comments, polls, and forums. Likewise, Thurman [45] analyses ten large British newspaper sites for the type of user-generated content (comments, polls, chat rooms, etc.). Some non-peer-reviewed sources offer a general overview of the available amount of comment spaces available. According to Thomä [44], in 2008, around 42% of German newspapers, which had an online presence, offered comment sections. A year later, Neuberger [31] measured that amount to 65%. However, while Thomä [44] analysed comment functions, Neuberger [31] searched for discussion forums. Therefore, the two figures cannot be compared directly. As the most recent contribution, the dissertation of Zimmermann [49] depicts the 35 largest German news-outlets and found 83% offering comment sections, a figure which corresponds well to our findings (Sect. 4).

Apart from the mentioned sources, we did not find any structured overview over the comment sections of both English or German newspapers to the best of our efforts.

3 Method

To provide additional and novel information to the previously published interview or survey pieces (e.g., [40]), we conducted a structured assessment of the webpages of the individual newspapers and additional meta data. To achieve this, we first selected a sample of German newspapers to analyse in our research (see Sect. 3.1). Secondly, we collected a set of criteria for each of the identified newspapers (see Sect. 3.2).

3.1 Sample Selection

The first step to start our research was to establish a ground truth of newspapers to work with. As the news landscape of Germany is complex and broken down into various news outlets of local, regional, and national interest, we procured a list of all active newspapers from the German Newspaper Publishers and Digitalpublishers Association[1]—the official association of newspaper publishers in Germany. The list encompasses 598 titles as of 1st February 2021. The list is enhanced by a substantial amount of additional meta data such as the type of paid content, special interests, and the URL of the newspaper (the only relevant data point for our research). Iterating through the data, it became clear that the data is not processable without further filtering, as several newspapers listed were only clones of other newspapers, and several of the listed outlets seemed too local to be of relevance. Against this backdrop, the following filters were applied:

- all advertisement papers (in German typically called "Anzeiger") were removed, as they usually do not constitute news media but rather news-enhanced advertisement
- newspapers sharing the same top-level domain (TLD) were reduced to the newspaper being primarily attached to this TLD (filtering of duplicates)

After these criteria were applied, we were left with a sample of 270 individual newspapers. To have additional filtering criteria available we complemented the available list with the publicly available media data of each listed outlet. Media data are information for advertisers published by the newspapers or their publishers, which typically include information regarding their circulation and the dominant regions of the newspaper. Despite the availability of website data for many newspapers, we decided to go for the print circulation[2] as the relevant

---

[1] official German name: *Bundesverband Digitalpublisher und Zeitungsverleger* (BDZV); https://www.bdzv.de/.

[2] To normalise different amounts of publishing days only circulations from Monday to Friday were taken into consideration.

locality criterion. The problem with website data is that the computation methods vary and clicks might be inflated if the newspaper website offers additional functionality like a job market. Based on an initial assessment of the print circulations, we decided to filter out super local newspapers with circulations lower than 30,000. This reduced our sample size to 114 newspapers. A check for the adequacy of the sample size to cover the overall sample of 270 newspapers with the confidence of 95% and an error rate of 10% indicates that 72 items would have been sufficient—a number we are surpassing by 42 items.

3.2 Analysed Aspects

After selecting the newspapers, we had to determine the data points to collect for further analysis. The collection follows the general idea of web content analysis [21]: We inspected each of the 114 newspaper websites and checked the individual aspects.

The central aspect of interest was the options for reader participation. Here we distinguished between three options: letters to the editor, surveys, and the comment sections—where the latter were at the heart of our analysis (cf., [25] and Sect. 4 for reasons for the importance of comment sections). For this, all websites were listed as offering comment sections that offer these either per article, for a selection of articles, or only offer aggregated, commentable articles (e.g., Süddeutsche Zeitung). External, non-embedded commenting options (e.g., Twitter) were not considered, being outside of the newspapers' governance area.

Furthermore, we surveyed the requirements for creating comments on the individual websites. For each newspaper website we tested, whether posting without any registration was possible or if registering was required. Whenever registrations were necessary we distinguished whether it could be done anonymous, if it required clear names or social media accounts, or even a paid account. This follows reports of [24] that high hurdles might increase civility. The requirements were checked through the terms of services and—where required—through registration attempts on the individual newspaper webpages.

Linked with this, we surveyed whether the corresponding outlet has codified regulations regarding their comment sections. Whenever codified regulations are present, we checked whether commenters are made aware nearby the comment section (at write time) or only in the terms and conditions (at registration time).

For each comment section, we also collected information regarding the implementation (self-developed or plug-in solution) and existing options to interact with the comments of others: Is it possible to answer to existing comments, rate, or report them? We finally determined whether a newspaper opted to go for pre- or post-moderation through experimentation with test comments.

4   Analysis

4.1   General Findings

Based on the collected data, the first finding is that 87% ($n = 99$) of the assessed newspapers still offer at least one option for reader participation. In Fig. 1 the distribution of these options is broken down further: The most common participatory feature is the comment section with 63 observations ($\sim$55% of the sampled newspapers), closely followed by the traditional letters to the editor with 59 observations ($\sim$ 52%), and a bit detached, surveys with only 39 observations ($\sim$35%). While combinations of different participatory features exist, they are comparatively rare with not more than 30 newspapers, e.g., offering comment sections and letters to the editor. A combination of all options only happens in 13 instances.

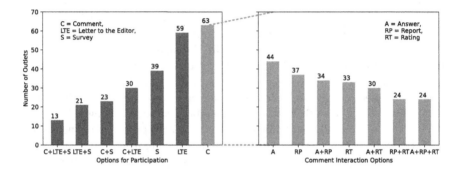

Fig. 1. Options for participation and comment interaction options

As comment sections allow more than a one-directional interaction of the user with the newspaper, we further assessed which interaction and feedback options publishers give to the users of their comment sections. Here the vast majority allows their readers to engage with other readers' comments. Primarily, this happens through an "Answer"-option (44 observations; $\sim$70%) and the ability to report problematic posts (37 observations; $\sim$59%). Rating of other people's post is the least popular option, only implemented 33 times ($\sim$52%). Differing from the options for participation, options are typically combined: the combination of reporting and answering are observed 34 times ($\sim$54%), and even the combination of all three options can be counted 24 times ($\sim$38%).

While the internet generally allows for anonymous participation, all of the analysed newspapers prohibit commenting without any prior registration (cf., Fig. 2). The second lowest hurdle, registering with a nickname, is only allowed by the minority of newspapers ($n = 14/22\%$), while the absolute majority requires their audience to give them their full names. Approximately half of these outlets ($n = 21/34\%$) only require registering with full/clear names and address data, which, however, still leaves room for the creation of fake accounts. In our tests,

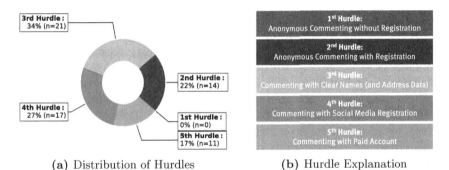

(a) Distribution of Hurdles   **(b)** Hurdle Explanation

Fig. 2. Application of commenting hurdles (incl. explanation) in the analysed 63 newspapers with comment sections

only one of the newspapers deleted our fake profile because the provided address data was found to be incorrect[3]. While this step is tailored to link peoples' opinions to their real identities, the leeway for anonymity is still massive. To encounter this, 17 newspapers (27%) force their audience to register with their social media account. Finally, 11 newspapers (17%) only allow the creation of comments for paying customers. An approach that, based on discussion with industry experts, seems to gain popularity in the future, as it is the most reliable way to identify people safely.

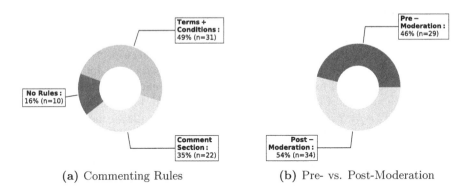

(a) Commenting Rules   **(b)** Pre- vs. Post-Moderation

Fig. 3. Moderation guidelines and enforcement

As indicated in Fig. 3a, newspapers do not only require their readers to register to become active participants—the majority also subjects them to rules and guidelines regarding how to comment. 53 newspapers—84% of the analysed set—have rules in place that regulate the code of conduct; only 10 (16%) let

---

[3] The *Badische Zeitung* blocks profiles created with data such as "Musterstraße 13" ("Sample Street 13") and "Musterhausen; PLZ 12345" ("Sample City; ZIP: 12345").

their audience act unrestricted. While almost 50% of the outlets use the "traditional" terms and conditions approach to implementing rules, 22 newspapers (35%) implement a more visible approach: They display parts of the rules as short texts or symbols close to the commenting area to remind their audience of the code of conduct on every commenting occasion. We even discovered commenting regulations in the terms and conditions of four newspapers that were not offering comment sections at the time of analysis. The two available moderation policies to enforce commenting guidelines are almost evenly split (cf., Fig. 3b). However, the stricter pre-moderation is applied slightly less often, with 29 outlets using it (46%), while 34 outlets (54%) opted for a post-moderation of their comments.

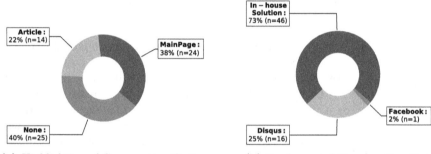

(a) Highlighting of Commenting Option   (b) Implemented Commenting Tool

Fig. 4. Implementation specifics of the used commenting solutions

Further, we analysed whether the newspapers highlight respectively advertise their comment sections to their users—or whether it is a rather hidden feature. The majority has small indicators showing the availability of comment sections and often the number of comments. Typically, these can be found on their main landing pages ($n = 24/38\%$). Alternatively, 14 outlets (22%) indicate this on the respective article pages. The remaining 25 newspapers (40%) decided not to visually highlight the existence of comments at all. To conclude our analysis, we had a look on the implementation of the comment sections. Only 17 newspapers (27%) use a recognisable foreign implementation, with *Disqus* being the leading third-party implementation. Most newspapers resort to custom or more proprietary solutions that come with their content management systems or have been self-programmed—these have been subsumed as "in-house solutions" in Fig. 4.

4.2   Findings by Newspaper Size

To analyse the impact of newspaper size on the participation offering we further analysed data we gathered—as described in Sect. 3.1—according to their circulation numbers. The range of sold copies lies between 1.2 million (*Bild*[4]) and 1,050

---

[4] https://www.bild.de.

copies (*Borkumer Zeitung*[5]). The share of newspapers that have a total circulation of more than over 30K copies is 47%. The distribution of the newspapers and the group sizes are shown in Fig. 5. The x-axis shows the newspapers studied, represented as dots. The names of the newspapers have been omitted for the sake of readability. The y-axis shows in increments of 100K that only two newspapers have a circulation higher than 300K copies. Under a sold circulation of 300K, the distribution continues evenly to the right, observing that the majority of newspapers have a paid circulation of less than 100K copies. The paid circulation figures of the newspapers follow a characteristic long-tail distribution, whereby a few newspaper copies have a very high circulation and thus represent a mass product [7]. In order to analyse the impact of newspaper circulation numbers on the user-participation opportunities, we grouped the newspapers based on their circulation numbers. For this reason, newspapers were counted in the first group of high circulation (HC) with a paid circulation of 150K or more. The second group, medium circulation (MC), newspapers with a paid circulation between 150K and 50K were added. The last group, small circulation (SC), contains all newspapers with a paid circulation of less than 50K copies. The subsets consist of the sample sizes HC with $n = 23$, MC with $n = 59$, and SC with $n = 32$ newspapers examined.

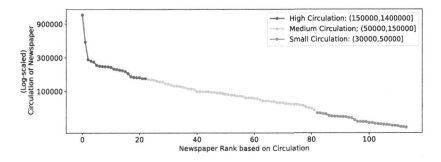

Fig. 5. Log-scaled newspaper circulation numbers

The first consideration of the groups is done via the relative shares of the three characteristics, participation opportunity, positioning of the comment section, and rules & regulations, which are listed in Table 1. The proportion of at least one participation option offered is very high in all three groups. It can be seen that almost every newspaper in the SC group offers one of the three participation options. This high value occurs due to the fact that SC offers the most comment sections with 63% and polls with 47%. The HC group only offers the most letters to the editor. Comment sections are not even implemented by half of all outlets the in the HC group. The MC group has similar figures for comment sections and letters to the editors to those of the other two groups. In the survey metric, the share of 24% deviates more strongly from the other results.

---

[5] https://www.borkumer-zeitung.de.

Table 1. Relative share of selected characteristics in the groups high circulation (HC), medium circulation (MC), and small circulation (SC)

	HC	MC	SC
Participation opportunities			
Comment sections	48%	54%	63%
Letter to the editors	65%	49%	47%
Polls	43%	24%	47%
Opportunities offered	83%	85%	97%
Positioning of comment section			
Below article	72%	53%	75%
Comment section rules			
Are available	81%	86%	80%
Positioning next to comment section	66%	54%	62%

5   Discussion

Given the lack of quantitative studies and the rising amount of research setting forth to find ways to semi-automate comment moderation, we created a structured overview of the German comment landscape using a substantial sample of 114 newspaper websites. Germany serves as a typical example of a country being caught between maintaining free speech and restraining illegal speech.

Despite many disheartening articles of both scholarly and journalistic nature outlining the failure and demise of comment sections [15,23], our analysis indicates that comment sections are still active for 63% of the analysed outlets and are even the preferred means for audience engagement in Germany—at least from the perspective of the offering side. In our sample, the option to post comments even outranks the traditional and still well-accepted letter to the editor. This is a strong indication that comment sections are still perceived as a valid or required format by many newspapers [1]. The fact that 83% of all assessed newspapers offer comment sections for free is a further indication that even without directly generated income, comment sections are economically viable—and in 60% of the cases even advertised on the main page or the article page itself. While recent reports indicate that only between 10% and 23% of the German newspaper audience regularly use comment sections [22,48], roughly 42% are reading comments at least once per week [48]. In this regard, the anticipated audience is extant and substantial enough to support the observed behaviour of the newspapers. One reason for this observed behaviour might be the increasing focus on audience engagement, which is often measured by time spent on a news page, page clicks, and interactions and is often used to determine advertisement revenue [12,30,41].

Furthermore, the higher share of comment sections in smaller—and hence typically more local—newspapers align with observations made by other researchers: Local journalism is considered to be one of the rising concepts in journalism—and one where connecting with the audience is both easiest and most promising [30]. One reason, according to Nelson [30], might be the rising focus on what he calls "production-oriented journalism". Production-oriented journalism ascribes the audience an active role in the creation of news content, and especially for local news people have been found to be interested in this kind of engagement [30,42,43]. One potential problem of this development is that Su et al. [43] observed local newspapers to be most seriously affected by problematic comments while at the same time experiencing the higher economic pressures (which eventually will affect moderation as well).

Upon closer inspection, it stands out that newspapers are not very inclined to combine multiple options to *engage with their audience*. Only 13% use comments, letters to the editor, and surveys; the share at max. increases to 30% for comments and letters to the editor. This reflects observations and theories from the literature depicting journalists' eagerness for engagement as rather low [28]. Sometimes engagement is even seen as an unwanted management task and a burden—especially when comment sections are involved [1,25,38]. However, when it comes to facilitating *audience-internal engagement* newspapers seem to be more open, as more than 50% of the newspapers enabling such interaction also allow for a combination of all analysed forms (answering, reporting, rating). This partially maps with the prior observations that journalists rather leave the comment sections to the audience, with some even perceiving them as a form of sub-communities/external communities [6].

To account for some of the management and moderation efforts generated through online participation, none of the assessed German newspapers allow for anonymous commenting without registration—and only 22% allow for anonymous commenting with registration. This is considerably less than observed in the US, where up to 40% of the outlets still accept this mode of interaction [39]. The lower share and the observed regular enforcement of clear name registration or even the use of social media make sense against the backdrop of the results of [24,39]. They point out that reducing anonymity is a key factor to reducing incivility, which, however, should be carefully considered, as authors such as Su et al. [43] identified this effect to be non-existent. In line with this we found the majority of newspapers provide guidelines for their audiences explicitly outlining allowed and disallowed behaviour. 35% of the observed outlets even apply digital nudging [47] through the placement of guidelines near the comment sections to ensure a more civil discussion environment. The fact that 54% still decide to post-moderate their comments is, however, conflicting. Post-moderation is comparatively risky, as abusive comments might be online for multiple hours before deletion [46]. This is why authors such as [24] linked post-moderation with increased incivility. However, as pre-moderation is typically more resource-intensive than post-moderation [24,46] many outlets might resort to the cheaper option to be able to offer comments at all. Hence, the increasing work on automation and decision support for comment moderation and community management [16,33] is well justified and might turn out beneficial in keeping comment sections alive.

6 Conclusion and Limitations

By assessing 114 German newspaper websites and analysing the extant options for user participation, associated hurdles, and limitations, we provided the, to our knowledge, most extensive, quantitative overview of this kind. While it could be shown that comment sections—against the trend five years ago—are still extant and important, we found out that German newspapers are so far mostly trying to restrict incivility by implementing hurdles to comment. Regarding the moderation policies and the nudging of audiences, there is still room for improvement—and/or automation. Especially for large outlets, there appears to be a need for development, as they dropped comment sections more often than their smaller counterparts.

However, our study is not without limitations or areas for extension. While the quantitative approach helped establish a neutral and objective picture of the commenting and participatory landscape in German newspapers, it methodologically cannot deliver insights into the "why" behind the status quo. Based on the numbers outlined in this paper, future research could elaborate on reasons for dropping comment sections, justifications for post-moderation, etc., by complementing the statistics with interview data. Furthermore, Germany is not the only country affected by incivility and the closing of comment sections. Hence, similar studies for other countries caught in the conflict zone of free speech and abusiveness—such as the US, the UK, or the Scandinavian countries—would make excellent candidates for further quantitative studies complementing the picture outlined in this paper. Last but not least, the sketched method could serve as a basis for regular updates to better monitor the state of participatory options in the future.

Acknowledgments. The research leading to these results received funding from the federal state of North Rhine-Westphalia and the European Regional Development Fund (EFRE.NRW 2014–2020), Project: M●DERAT! (No. CM-2-2-036a).

References

1. Bergström, A., Wadbring, I.: Beneficial yet crappy: journalists and audiences on obstacles and opportunities in reader comments. Eur. J. Commun. **30**(2), 137–151 (2015)
2. Bilton, R.: Why some publishers are killing their comment sections (2014). https://digiday.com/media/comments-sections/
3. Binns, A.: Don't feed the trolls!: managing troublemakers in magazines' online communities. J. Pract. **6**(4), 547–562 (2012)
4. Boberg, S., Schatto-Eckrodt, T., Frischlich, L., Quandt, T.: The moral gatekeeper? Moderation and deletion of user-generated content in a leading news forum. Media Commun. **6**(4), 58–69 (2018)
5. Bowman, S., Willis, C.: We media: how audiences are shaping the future of news and information (2003)
6. Bruns, A.: Making audience engagement visible: publics for journalism on social media platforms. 1st edn. chap. 33, pp. 325–334. Routledge, London (2016)

7. Brynjolfsson, E.: From niches to riches: anatomy of the long tail. MIT Sloan Manag. Rev. **47**(4), 67–71 (2006)

8. Canter, L.: The misconception of online comment threads: content and control on local newspaper websites. J. Pract. **7**(5), 604–619 (2013)

9. Chatley, R., Eisenbach, S., Magee, J.: Modelling a framework for plugins Robert. In: Barnett, M., Edwards, S.H., Giannakopoulou, D., Leavens, G.T. (eds.) Specification and Verification of Component-Based Systems, SAVCBS 2003, Helsinki, Finland, pp. 49–57 (2003)

10. Coe, K., Kenski, K., Rains, S.A.: Online and uncivil? Patterns and determinants of incivility in newspaper website comments. J. Commun. **64**(4), 658–679 (2014)

11. Cooper, C., Knotts, H.G., Haspel, M.: The content of political participation: letters to the editor and the people who write them. PS - Polit. Sci. Polit. **42**(1), 131–137 (2009)

12. Costera Meijer, I.: Understanding the audience turn in journalism: from quality discourse to innovation discourse as anchoring practices 1995–2020. Journal. Stud. **21**(16), 2326–2342 (2020). https://doi.org/10.1080/1461670X.2020.1847681

13. Domingo, D., Quandt, T., Heinonen, A., Paulussen, S., Singer, J.B., Vujnovic, M.: Participatory journalism practices in the media and beyond: an international comparative study of initiatives in online newspapers. Journal. Pract. **2**(3), 326–342 (2008)

14. Einwiller, S.A., Kim, S.: How online content providers moderate user-generated content to prevent harmful online communication: an analysis of policies and their implementation. Policy Internet **12**(2), 184–206 (2020)

15. Ellis, J.: What happened after 7 news sites got rid of reader comments, September 2015. https://www.niemanlab.org/2015/09/what-happened-after-7-news-sites-got-rid-of-reader-comments/

16. Fortuna, P., Nunes, S.: A survey on automatic detection of hate speech in text. ACM Comput. Surv. **51**(4), 1–30 (2018)

17. Frischlich, L., Boberg, S., Quandt, T.: Comment sections as targets of dark participation? Journalists' evaluation and moderation of deviant user comments. J. Stud. **20**(14), 2014–2033 (2019)

18. Gardiner, B., Mansfield, M., Anderson, I., Holder, J., Louter, D., Ulmanu, M.: The dark side of Guardian comments (2016). https://www.theguardian.com/technology/2016/apr/12/the-dark-side-of-guardian-comments

19. Gerpott, T.J., Schlegel, M.: Online-zeitungen: charakteristika und anwendungspotenziale eines neuen medienangebots. M&K Medien Kommunikationswissenschaft **48**(3), 335–353 (2000)

20. Hayek, L., Mayrl, M., Russmann, U.: The citizen as contributor-letters to the editor in the Austrian Tabloid Paper Kronen Zeitung (2008–2017). J. Stud. **21**(8), 1127–1145 (2020)

21. Herring, S.C.: Web content analysis: expanding the paradigm. In: Hunsiger, J., Klastrup, L., Allen, M. (eds.) International Handbook of Internet Research, pp. 233–249. Springer, Heidelberg (2010). https://doi.org/10.1007/978-1-4020-9789-8_14

22. Höllig, S., Hasebrink, U.: Reuters institute digital news report 2020 – Ergebnisse für Deutschland. Technical report, Leibniz-Institut für Medienforschung–Hans-Bredow-Institut (HBI), Hamburg, Germany (2020)

23. Juarez Miro, C.: The comment gap: affective publics and gatekeeping in The New York Times' comment sections. Journalism 1–17 (2020)

24. Ksiazek, T.B.: Civil interactivity: how news organizations' commenting policies explain civility and hostility in user comments. J. Broadcast. Electron. Media **59**(4), 556–573 (2015)
25. Loosen, W., et al.: Making sense of user comments: identifying journalists' requirements for a comment analysis framework. Stud. Commun. Media **6**(4), 333–364 (2017)
26. Loosen, W., Schmidt, J.H.: Between proximity and distance: including the audience in journalism (research). In: Franklin, B., Eldridge, S.A. (eds.) Routledge Companion to Digital Journalism Studies, 1st edn., chap. 35, pp. 354–363. Routledge, London (2016)
27. Meyer, H.K., Carey, M.C.: In moderation: examining how journalists' attitudes toward online comments affect the creation of community. J. Pract. **8**(2), 213–228 (2014)
28. Mitchelstein, E.: Catharsis and community: divergent motivations for audience participation in online newspapers and blogs. Int. J. Commun. **5**(1), 2014–2034 (2011)
29. Muddiman, A., Stroud, N.J.: News values, cognitive biases, and partisan incivility in comment sections. J. Commun. **67**(4), 586–609 (2017)
30. Nelson, J.L.: The next media regime: the pursuit of 'audience engagement' in journalism. Journalism 1–18 (2019). https://doi.org/10.1177/1464884919862375
31. Neuberger, C.: Journalismus in der netzwerköffentlichkeit. In: Nuernbergk, C., Neuberger, C. (eds.) Journalismus im Internet, pp. 11–80. Springer, Wiesbaden (2018). https://doi.org/10.1007/978-3-531-93284-2_2
32. Nielsen, R.K.: Participation through letters to the editor: circulation, considerations, and genres in the letters institution. Journalism **11**(1), 21–35 (2010)
33. Niemann, M., Welsing, J., Riehle, D.M., Brunk, J., Assenmacher, D., Becker, J.: Abusive comments in online media and how to fight them. In: van Duijn, M., Preuss, M., Spaiser, V., Takes, F., Verberne, S. (eds.) MISDOOM 2020. LNCS, vol. 12259, pp. 122–137. Springer, Cham (2020). https://doi.org/10.1007/978-3-030-61841-4_9
34. Nip, J.Y.: Exploring the second phase of public journalism. Journal. Stud. **7**(2), 212–236 (2006)
35. Nobata, C., Tetreault, J., Thomas, A., Mehdad, Y., Chang, Y.: Abusive language detection in online user content. In: Proceedings of 25th International Conference World Wide Web, WWW 2016, pp. 145–153. ACM Press, Montreal (2016)
36. Pöyhtäri, R.: Limits of hate speech and freedom of speech on moderated news websites in Finland, Sweden, The Netherlands and the UK. Annales-Ser. Hist. Sociol. izhaja štirikrat letno **24**(3), 513–524 (2014)
37. Reich, Z.: User comments. Participatory journalism: guarding open gates at online newspapers, pp. 96–117 (2011)
38. Robinson, S.: Traditionalists vs. convergers: textual privilege, boundary work, and the journalist-audience relationship in the commenting policies of online news sites. Convergence **16**(1), 125–143 (2010)
39. Santana, A.D.: Virtuous or Vitriolic: the effect of anonymity on civility in online newspaper reader comment boards. J. Pract. **8**(1), 18–33 (2014)
40. Siegert, S.: Nahezu jede zweite Zeitungsredaktion schränkt Online-Kommentare ein (2016). http://www.journalist.de/aktuelles/meldungen/journalist-umfrage-nahezu-jede-2-zeitungsredaktion-schraenkt-onlinekommentare-ein.html
41. Steensen, S., Ferrer-Conill, R., Peters, C.: (Against a) theory of audience engagement with news. J. Stud. **21**(12), 1662–1680 (2020). https://doi.org/10.1080/1461670X.2020.1788414

42. Stroud, N.J., Duyn, E.V., Peacock, C.: News commenters and news comment readers. Technical report, Engaging News Project (2016). https://engagingnewsproject.org/enp_prod/wp-content/uploads/2016/03/ENP-News-Commenters-and-Comment-Readers1.pdf

43. Su, L.Y.F., Xenos, M.A., Rose, K.M., Wirz, C., Scheufele, D.A., Brossard, D.: Uncivil and personal? Comparing patterns of incivility in comments on the Facebook pages of news outlets. New Media Soc. 20(10), 3678–3699 (2018). https://doi.org/10.1177/1461444818757205

44. Thomä, M.: Der Zerfall des Publikums: Nachrichtennutzung zwischen Zeitung und Internet. Springer, Heidelberg (2013). https://doi.org/10.1007/978-3-658-03646-1

45. Thurman, N.: Forums for citizen journalists? Adoption of user generated content initiatives by online news media. New Media Soc. 10(1), 139–157 (2008)

46. Veglis, A.: Moderation techniques for social media content. In: Meiselwitz, G. (ed.) SCSM 2014. LNCS, vol. 8531, pp. 137–148. Springer, Cham (2014). https://doi.org/10.1007/978-3-319-07632-4_13

47. Weinmann, M., Schneider, C., vom Brocke, J.: Digital nudging. Bus. Inf. Syst. Eng. 58(6), 433–436 (2016)

48. Ziegele, M., Springer, N., Jost, P., Wright, S.: Online user comments across news and other content formats: multidisciplinary perspectives, new directions. Stud. Commun. Media 6(4), 315–332 (2017)

49. Zimmermann, T.: Digitale Diskussionen: Über politische Partizipation mittels Online-Leserkommentaren, vol. 44. Transcript Verlag (2017)

Evaluating the Role of News Content and Social Media Interactions for Fake News Detection

Catherine Sotirakou(✉) ⓘ, Anastasia Karampela ⓘ,
and Constantinos Mourlas ⓘ

Faculty of Communication and Media Studies,
National and Kapodistrian University of Athens, Athens, Greece
{katerinasot,anakaram,mourlas}@media.uoa.gr

Abstract. Societies across the globe suffer from the effects of disinformation campaigns creating an urgent need for a way of tracking falsehoods before they become widely spread. Although building a detection tool for online disinformation campaigns is a challenging task, this paper attempts to approach this problem by examining content-based features related to language use, emotions, and engagement features through explainable machine learning. We propose a model that, except for the textual attributes, harnesses the predictive power of the users' interactions on the Facebook platform, and forecasts deceptive content in (i) news articles and in (ii) Facebook news-related posts. The findings of the study show that the proposed model is able to predict misleading news stories with a 98% accuracy based on features such as capitals in the main body, headline length, Facebook likes, the total amount of nouns and numbers, lexical diversity, and arousal. In conclusion, the paper provides new insights concerning the false news identifiers crucial for both news publishers and consumers.

Keywords: Fake news detection · Disinformation · Fact-checking · Digital journalism · Natural language processing · Machine learning · Explainable AI

1 Introduction

The intentional spread of false and concocted information serves many purposes such as financial and political interests, influencing public discourse against marginalized populations, has a negative impact on society and democracy [16,30], and can expose the public to immediate danger. Examples of false stories that went viral on social media platforms like the "Pizzagate", a conspiracy theory that threatened the lives of the employees of a pizzeria [29] and coronavirus-related false content that led people to drink toxic chemicals with at least 800 people dead and thousands hospitalized[1], show that online virality can become

---

[1] https://www.bbc.com/news/world-53755067.

© Springer Nature Switzerland AG 2021
J. Bright et al. (Eds.): MISDOOM 2021, LNCS 12887, pp. 128–141, 2021.
https://doi.org/10.1007/978-3-030-87031-7_9

dangerous. More specifically, previous research has found that social bots are crucial in the spread of misinformation [27] since search engines, social media platforms, and news aggregators use algorithms that control the information a user sees. For instance, algorithmic curation on Google can promote a greatly visited news article very high on the search results, thus improving the likelihood of it being shared, read, and emailed. Audience metrics such as page views, likes, shares, and so on, unquestionably influence the number of people who see a given article on their screen. Therefore, experts in disinformation and online radicalization take advantage of these known algorithmic vulnerabilities by creating fabricated accounts which generate fake traffic that results in virality [27]. Virality in turn guarantees that disinformation, trolling rumors, and coordinated campaigns are rapidly propagated across the internet, and as Lotan [12] highlights what we need is "algorithms that optimize for an informed public, rather than page views and traffic". Nevertheless, after much debate about the need for Facebook to change its algorithm to reduce filter bubbles, and the platform's avoidance of taking responsibility for the distribution of deceptive content on its News Feed, since mid-December 2016 it started to alter its algorithm to make misleading information to appear lower and Google followed with raising the fact-checked stories higher [3]. However, the Covid-19 pandemic proved those measures were insufficient, while also highlighting the challenges that journalists face as they need to manually check countless requests of potentially deceptive information daily[2], without sometimes possessing the necessary skills, or having the resources, time, and expert personnel to fight disinformation [3].

The urgent need for disinformation detection led many scientific disciplines in the search for new effective ways to mitigate this problem with promising approaches coming from various fields. In line with this, this paper proposes a computational approach to detect potentially fake information, by identifying textual and nontextual characteristics of both fake and real news articles and then using machine learning algorithms for disinformation prediction. More precisely, we consider two sets of machine-readable features i) content-based, and ii) engagement-based, and we conduct our analysis in two distinct phases. In phase A, only content-based features are explored, while in phase B we add features that correspond to the users' interactions on Facebook and test them on a subset of the original fake and real news dataset.

2   Related Work

Fake and manipulated information is circulated in all forms and platforms, unverified videos are shared on Facebook, rumors are being forwarded via messaging apps, while conspiracy theories are being shared by Twitter influencers, and these are only a few of the distribution patterns of disinformation. According to Tandoc and his colleagues [32] the role of social media platforms is crucial to understand the current state of disinformation globally since Facebook and Twitter changed both the news distribution and the trust to traditional media

---

[2] https://www.poynter.org/coronavirusfactsalliance/.

outlets. As they vividly note "now, a tweet, which at most is 140 characters long, is considered a piece of news, particularly if it comes from a person in authority" [32]. In this work, we consider real news as defined by Kovach and Rosenstiel [11] to be "independent, reliable, accurate, and comprehensive information", and "not include unverified facts", thus disinformation campaigns threaten to curtail the actual purpose of journalism, which is "to provide citizens with the information they need to be free and self-governing" [11]. In addition, to define fake news we use the description by the European Commission [5] "disinformation is understood as verifiably false or misleading information that is created, presented, and disseminated for economic gain or to intentionally deceive the public, and may cause public harm". Journalists and professional fact-checkers can determine the correctness of potential threats based on their expertise and the use of many digital tools designed to detect a plethora of manipulated elements inside a fake story. Finally, news verification can be a procedure done inside a news outlet that checks all the information before publication or it can be done after the piece is published or shared in social media networks.

The rise of disinformation has attracted strong interest from computer scientists who employ machine learning and other automated methods to help identify disinformation. Fake news detection in computer science is defined as the task of classifying news by its veracity [19] with many studies of this phenomenon aiming to extract useful linguistic and other types of features and then build effective models that can identify and predict fake news from real content. A useful overview of the computational methods used for automated disinformation detection [6] separates two categories, notably machine learning research using linguistic cues, and network analysis using behavioral data. In this section, we will focus only on previous work around the former category, linguistic approaches.

The thought behind linguistic approaches for fake news detection based on content is to find predictive deception elements which can lead to distinguishing the fakeness of news [25]. Rubin et al. [25] built a Support Vector Machine (SVM) model to identify satire and humor articles. Their model performed with 87% accuracy and the results showed that the best predictive features were absurdity, grammar, and punctuation. A similar study from Horne and Adali [9] compared real news against satire articles using also SVM with an accuracy of 91%, and found that headlines, complexity, and style of content are good predictors of satire news. However, when classifying real and fake news the accuracy dropped dramatically. Ahmed et al. [1] experimented with n-grams and examined different feature extraction methods and multiple machine learning models, to find the best algorithm to classify disinformation. The results showed that overall linear-based classifiers are better than nonlinear ones, with the highest accuracy achieved by a Linear SVM. Furthermore, Shu et al. [30] conducted a survey providing a comprehensive review of fake news detection on social media. They discussed existing fake news detection approaches from a data mining perspective, including feature extraction, model construction, and evaluation metrics.

For the fake news corpuses, many researchers use ready-to-use datasets, such as BuzzFeedNews[3], BuzzFace[4], BS Detector[5], CREDBANK[6] and FacebookHoax[7] [29] and others construct their own using potentially false stories from websites marked as fake news by PolitiFact [2,34]. Wang et al. [34] introduced LIAR, a benchmark dataset for fake news detection about politics created from manually labeled reports from Politifact.com. In this work, the authors used a Convolutional Neural Network and showed that the combination of meta-data with text improves disinformation detection. Asubario and Rubin, [2] downloaded fabricated articles from websites marked as fake news sources by PolitiFact.com and matched them with real news around the same political topics. Their computational content analysis showed that false political news articles tend to have fewer words and paragraphs than the real ones although the fabricated stories have lengthier paragraphs and include more profanity and affectivity. Finally, the titles of the fake stories are bigger and more emotional, including more punctuation marks, demonstratives, and fewer verifiable facts.

Several studies related to fake news detection examined social media aiming to extract useful features and build effective models that can differentiate potentially fabricated stories over truthful news. The study of Tacchini et al. [31] focused on whether a hoax post can be identified based on how many people "liked" it on Facebook. Using two different classification techniques, which both provided a performance of 99% accuracy, the research proved that hoax posts have, on average, more likes than non-hoax posts, indicating that the users' interactions on news posts on social media platforms can be used to predict whether posts are hoaxes. Similarly, the study of Idrees et al. [10] showed that the users' reactions to Facebook news-related posts are an important factor for determining if they are fake or not. The authors proposed a model based on both users' comments and expressed emotions (emoji) and suggested that a future Support Vector Machine approach would increase its accuracy. Finally, the work of Reis et al. [24] examined features such as language use and source reliability, while also examining the social network structure. The authors studied the degree of users' engagement and the temporal patterns and evaluated the discriminative power of the features using several classifiers with the best results obtained by a Random Forest and an XGBoost which both had an F1 score of 81%.

In line with previous work in Communication and Computational Linguistics, this study proposes that the detection of disinformation campaigns can be examined in great detail if it is treated as a classification problem, leveraging explainable machine learning models that can provide new insights on how to identify potentially misleading information. Taking previous findings into consideration, we created a model that uses content-based and engagement features

---

[3] https://github.com/BuzzFeedNews/2016-10-facebook-fact-check/tree/master/data.

[4] https://github.com/gsantia/BuzzFace.

[5] https://github.com/bs-detector/bs-detector.

[6] http://compsocial.github.io/CREDBANK-data/.

[7] https://github.com/gabll/some-like-it-hoax.

as potential predictors of disinformation. Our goal is twofold, first to examine the effectiveness of the proposed model and second provide conclusions concerning which factors predict fake news stories and especially why particular characteristics of news articles are more important in classifying them as fake. Finding answers to these questions is crucial for journalists, editors, and the audience.

3   Model and Feature Extraction

The main purpose of this study is to create an inclusive model to detect disinformation campaigns in (i) news articles and in (ii) Facebook news-related posts. The backbone of the model is structured based on an extensive review of previous studies in both communication and computational linguistics. In the light of the literature, we identify the following types of features:

3.1   Content-Based Features

Linguistic: The length of the article and the length of the headline are considered good predictors for potentially false content [2,9], while the use of capitalized words in the body and title of the stories [4] along with certain POS tags such as nouns, demonstratives, personal pronouns, adverbs [2,9] help detect deceptive content. Furthermore, complexity measures like the level of lexical diversity and readability have been used in previous studies with lower levels of complexity to point to fake content [9]. Also, the high number of swear words increases the probability of an article being false [2].

Emotional: Emotionality is linked to disinformation in many studies [7,9] with false stories containing more negativity than real news [9] while provocative misleading content on social media has been found to express more anger in an effort to exasperate the audience [7]. In this study, we focus on two different aspects of emotionality to capture i) the actual emotion expressed in the text by measuring the intensity scores for anger, fear, sadness, joy, based on theories of basic emotions [21] and ii) the overall affect that includes the level of valence, arousal, and dominance as described by Russel [26]. The difference between emotion and affect is explained by [28], and defines the emotion as the demonstration of a feeling, whereas the intensity of the non-conscious response of the body to an experience relates to the affect.

3.2   Engagement Features

Facebook likes have been identified as significant predictors of hoaxes [24,31], and users' comments and reactions to Facebook news-related posts provide patterns that can point to disinformation [10]. Hereafter, the main features of our model are explained in detail along with the rationale for their selection in Table 1:

Table 1. Creation of the features.

Feature	Description
Content-based	
Linguistic	
Body length	The text size in characters. Real news articles are significantly longer than fake news articles [9]
Title length	The title size in characters. The total number of words in fake news titles is higher than in real news titles [9]
Capital letters in the story	In fake news articles are used more capitalized words [9]
Parts of speech	The identification of words as nouns, verbs, adverbs, adjectives, pronouns, prepositions, conjunctions, etc. The study [22] showed that words used to exaggerate, such as superlatives, and modal adverbs are indicative of fake news. However, the survey [14] indicated that trustworthy news writers tend to use more personal pronouns, proper nouns, adverbs, numbers [22] and name entities [25]
Noun/verb	The ratio of nouns to verbs in all words of the text [15]
Lexical Diversity	Refers to the ratio of different unique words in a text [9]
Readability	The Flesch readability score indicates how easy it is for someone to read a particular text, with high readability levels associated with real news [20]
Profanity	The number of swear words is a feature of fake news [9]
Title and body similarity	The relevance of content between the title and the main body, clickbait headlines are often different from the main story [33]
Subjectivity	The quality of news is characterized by the personal author's tone, and personal opinions expressed in a text [23]. Specifically, we measured the degree of weak or strong subjectivity using the MPQA Subjectivity Lexicon [35]
Emotional	
Emotions	For the emotion extraction, the NRC Affect Intensity Lexicon (NRC-AIL) was used that identifies the existence of four basic emotions, anger, fear, joy, and sadness [18]
Affect	We used NRC VAD Lexicon which identifies the sentiments of valence, arousal, and dominance [17]
Engagement	
Likes	The number of likes of the post [10]
Love	Represents more appreciation than liking and expresses more empathy [10]
Wow	Indicates a surprising feeling that the post expresses something unexpected [10]
Haha	Represents a funny reaction, the post causes real laughter or an ironic expression [10]
Sad	Shows sadness about the post's content also is a sign of refusal [10]
Angry	Represents the disliking of the post [10]
Shares	The number of shares may be related to news content truthfulness. [8]
Comments	The total number of comments
Total interactions	The total number of all interactions
Overperforming Score	The overperforming metric is calculated automatically by CrowdTangle[a] based on the performance of similar posts from the same page in similar timeframes

[a] https://help.crowdtangle.com/en/articles/3213537-crowdtangle-codebook.

4   Method and Dataset

For this study, we collected news articles from both trustworthy and unreliable English-language websites using the Python programming language. The dataset consists of a total of 23.420 articles both real and fake that were published online during the years 2019 and 2020, covering a variety of genres. This paper focuses only on the article level, therefore characteristics such as the overall likes or followers of a Facebook page and other contextual attributes like the genre were not taken into consideration. To construct the dataset, we followed the method of [2] and retrieved 12.420 articles from three widely acknowledged fake news websites, listed in many disinformation indexes such as PolitiFact's[8] fake news websites dataset and Wikipedia's list[9], namely, *dailysurge.com, dcgazette.com,* and *newspunch.com.* For real news, we collected a total of 11.000 articles from the following legitimate news sources: *nytimes.com, businessinsider.com, buzzfeed.com, newyorker.com, politico.com,* and *washingtonpost.com.* The articles cover various topics and include the article's full text, title, date, author, and web address (URL). The dependent variable was calculated by setting all stories scraped from fake websites the value of 1 and the truthful articles the value of 0. Furthermore, all articles were processed for stop-words, NaN values, stemming, tokenization, and lemmatization, while articles with less than 1K characters in the main body were deleted since a lot of the fake stories were very small. The total number of articles before the cleaning was 25.020, however, only 19.340 cases were qualified for consideration in the building of the model.

Furthermore, we gathered engagement data from Facebook, through the CrowdTangle platform that belongs to Facebook, and provides access to metrics about public pages and groups. More specifically, we searched for analytics for each article in our dataset published on Facebook using the same headline or URL. However, the query was not always successful because many articles did not appear on Facebook. Thus, we matched only 4822 fake news articles from the original dataset (from dailysurge.com, and newspunch.com.) with their corresponding Facebook metrics. Finally, to have a balanced dataset we included analytics for the same amount of real articles, resulting in a total of 9.644 articles for inclusion in the model.

For feature engineering, many Python libraries were used such as the py-readability-metrics[10] package and the Natural Language Toolkit[11] (NLTK) to perform basic text analysis and filtering. After the features of every category (content-based, engagement-based) were created, redundant features were identified by using a correlation matrix, and the ones with a correlation higher than 0.7

---

[8] https://www.politifact.com/article/2017/apr/20/politifacts-guide-fake-news-websites-and-what-they/.

[9] https://en.wikipedia.org/wiki/List_of_fake_news_websites.

[10] https://pypi.org/project/py-readability-metrics/.

[11] https://www.nltk.org/.

were removed from the data. Furthermore, several similar features were removed using clustering techniques. For the model, the Decision Tree and the Random Forest classifier from Scikit-learn Python library[12] were used, and we compared their results to find the one with the highest prediction accuracy. Afterward, the importance of each feature in this fake news classification problem was determined.

5   Data Analysis and Findings – In Two Distinctive Phases

For the data analysis, we separated the experiment into two phases based on the two different datasets. In Phase A, the original dataset was used for the evaluation of the importance of only the content-based features, notably the linguistic and emotional features. Then, in Phase B, a subset of the dataset that included Facebook activity (engagement features) was used twice. First, using only the engagement features as predictor variables, and then with all the features. The aim at this stage was to add the predictive power of the engagement features and check their effects on the accuracy scores. Furthermore, the overall goal of the analysis is to explore the different sets of features to be able to understand what elements of a story increase the probability of it being fake, thus we opted for models that are not complete black boxes but provide in-depth explanations of the classifier's predictions, such as tree-based models [13]. For all the experiments, 70% of the stories were used for training and the remaining 30% for testing, and three classification methods were used for the evaluation of the model, namely F-measure (F1), precision, and recall.

5.1   Phase A - Evaluating the Importance of the Proposed Model Content-Based Features

For phase A of the experiment, the original dataset (fake and real articles) was used to discover the most significant content-based features that can classify an article before publication, meaning that engagement features were not being considered at this stage. The two different classification methods were applied, and the algorithm with the highest accuracy was the Random Forest classifier with an F1-Score of 91%. Our main interest lies in the feature importances of the classifier that will enable us to interpret what matters most as the model constructs its decision trees, therefore except for calculating the contribution of every feature on the prediction (see Fig. 1), we also used the ELI5[13] Python package for "Inspecting Black-Box Estimators" to measure the permutation importance (Table 2).

---

[12] https://scikit-learn.org/stable/.
[13] https://eli5.readthedocs.io/en/latest/overview.html.

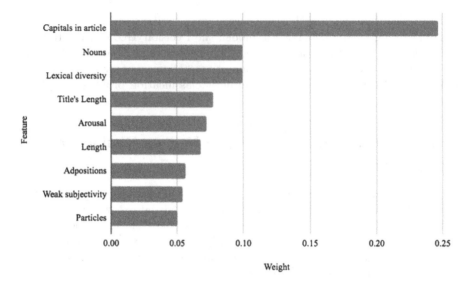

Fig. 1. Feature importance score for the content-based features

Figure 1 shows the importance of the content-based features. The category of linguistic features is the most significant with capital letters in the body of the article, POS tags (nouns, adpositions, particles), lexical diversity, headline length, article length, and weak subjectivity to be amongst the top-ten important predictors. From the emotional features, arousal is the only significant attribute for detecting false content.

5.2 Phase B - Combining the Content-Based Features with the Engagement Features

The objective of this phase is to examine if the combination of the textual characteristics of an article (content-based features), together with audience metrics (engagement features), provides better accuracy in distinguishing the fake from real news. In this stage, we used the smaller dataset that includes the engagement features, and ran the models twice; first, we examined the performance results based only on the engagement features, and then we combined all the features. The results of the two phases are presented in Table 3. When we ran the model the first time using only the engagement features, the random forest correctly classified 95.8% of news-related posts into either fake or real class, showing that even without any textual features such as headline length or lexical diversity the model performs well based on users' interactions with the Facebook platform. Furthermore, the total number of Facebook users who "liked" the post was the most important feature, followed by the overperforming score, calculated by CrowdTangle based on the performance of similar posts from the same page in similar timeframes.

Table 2. Permutation Importance for the top 10 combined features

Feature	Weight
Capitals in article	0.0758 ± 0.0095
Likes	0.0732 ± 0.0092
Title's Length	0.0595 ± 0.0038
Numbers	0.0190 ± 0.0045
Overperforming	0.0128 ± 0.0053
Arousal	0.0088 ± 0.0023
Nouns	0.0063 ± 0.0027
Comments	0.0049 ± 0.0033
Readability Score	0.0040 ± 0.0006
Strong Subjectivity	0.0040 ± 0.0016

Table 3. Accuracy of machine learning classifiers

Features	Measures in %	Machine Learning Classifiers	
		Decision Tree	Random Forest
News Content Features	Accuracy	84.1	91.0
Engagement Features	Accuracy	94.4	95.8
News Content Features + Engagement Features	Accuracy	94.9	98.0

As we can observe the combination of the content-based and engagement features proved to have greater predictive power compared to any single group of features. First on the top 3 of the permutation importance table (see Table 2) is the number of capital letters in the body of the article with the significance of this feature remaining stable in both datasets, while the second is the number of likes, followed by the length of the headline, which was very important also in phase A. Moreover, POS tags like numbers and nouns are significant predictors, while the overperforming score is the fifth most significant characteristic. Similar to phase A, arousal is the only emotional feature that contributes to the prediction, while the total number of comments a news post received, the readability score, and the expressed subjectivity are of lower importance.

6   Discussion of the Results

In general, as depicted in Table 2, the content-based features and especially the linguistic ones are the most informative for distinguishing real from fake news articles. The results are in line with previous studies [9, 15, 20, 22] which found that textual attributes can forecast the probability of a news item being deceptive. The second most important category of features is the engagement features, with the number of Likes being the best amongst them. Interestingly, the emotional category of features is third, (that belongs to content-based) with only the Arousal being significant for the prediction. The weights of the features show what matters most for the classifications and seem to relate well with the proposed categories of features.

Overall, the findings support several features recognized in studies methodologically close to this one. More specifically, features related to words in Capital letters were highlighted in the study of Horne and Adali [9], along with the Headline Length, and the Article Length that was significant also in the work of Marquardt [15]. Facebook Likes are essential for the model's predictions and have also been identified to distinguish hoax posts [24,31], and the use of the audience reactions on the platform considered to provide patterns that can point to disinformation [10]. Furthermore, our results show that the syntax of the fake news articles is very significant, and this is one of the features recognized by many researchers in the past, specifically, that false stories include more Adverbs [2,9,22], fewer Nouns [9,15], more personal Pronouns [2,20,22], fewer Numbers [22], and more demonstratives, [2]. Additionally, Lexical Diversity and Subjectivity proved to be significant in phase A in line with the findings of [9] that false stories have less lexical complexity and more self-referential words. On the contrary, characteristics often related to disinformation like profanity, negative sentiment [15] and anger [7] were not identified by the model as significant indicators of falsity.

7   Conclusion and Future Work

Many studies related to disinformation in news articles and social media treat fake news detection as a text classification problem, therefore extract features and build effective models that can predict false stories [6]. Accordingly, our study employed content-based and engagement features drawn from previous theoretical constructs in an attempt to model online disinformation campaigns and cast light on its significant identifiers. To this end, we created two datasets, one that included real and fake news and a subset of the original that contained the audience's interactions to the same articles posted on Facebook. Then we performed a number of experiments, comparing the different sets of features and two tree-based classifiers. Our findings revealed that the content-based features such as Capitals in the article, Headline Length, POS tags, and the engagement feature of Facebook Likes were the most important predictors of deceptive online stories. The results provided us with insights of fake news attributes useful in the light of combating disinformation, in terms of proposing a machine learning approach to automatically detect false stories and of pointing to certain telling characteristics of these falsehoods that could be incorporated in media literacy education programs to bolster resilience against this devastating phenomenon.

However, the results of this study are based on a set of assumptions producing the following limitations. First of all, the dataset was built based on the fundamental assumption that all the articles from the sources listed as fake news websites by Politifact are 100% fake. Undoubtedly, there are better ways of constructing a fake news corpus such as asking fact-checkers to verify the potentially deceptive stories before incorporating them into the dataset or opting for a human-in-the-loop approach where the model would not rely so heavily on Artificial intelligence but include more sophisticated human judgment. Except for the dependent variable of our model not being the optimal one, there is the limitation of the English language thus it is uncertain how the model would behave with datasets in other languages. Based on the current study, future work could use a more diverse dataset and design a study in which human fact-checkers define false stories based on certain features and their respective significance and then correlate their judgment with the feature importances of the model, or focus on rule extraction and investigate more closely the effect of each feature on disinformation detection.

Acknowledgements. The research work was supported by the Hellenic Foundation for Research and Innovation (HFRI) and the General Secretariat for Research and Technology (GSRT), under the HFRI PhD Fellowship grant (GA. 14540).

References

1. Ahmed, H., Traore, I., Saad, S.: Detection of online fake news using N-Gram analysis and machine learning techniques. In: Traore, I., Woungang, I., Awad, A. (eds.) ISDDC 2017. LNCS, vol. 10618, pp. 127–138. Springer, Cham (2017). https://doi.org/10.1007/978-3-319-69155-8_9
2. Asubiaro, T.V., Rubin, V.L.: Comparing features of fabricated and legitimate political news in digital environments (2016–2017). Proc. Assoc. Inf. Sci. Technol. **55**(1), 747–750 (2018)
3. Bakir, V., McStay, A.: Fake news and the economy of emotions: problems, causes, solutions. Digit. J. **6**(2), 154–175 (2018)
4. Bradshaw, S., Howard, P.N., Kollanyi, B., Neudert, L.M.: Sourcing and automation of political news and information over social media in the united states, 2016–2018. Polit. Commun. **37**(2), 173–193 (2020)
5. Commission, E.: Joint communication to the European parliament, the European council, the European economic and social committee and the committee of the regions: action plan against disinformation (2018)
6. Conroy, N.K., Rubin, V.L., Chen, Y.: Automatic deception detection: methods for finding fake news. Proc. Assoc. Inf. Sci. Technol. **52**(1), 1–4 (2015)
7. Freelon, D., Lokot, T.: Russian twitter disinformation campaigns reach across the american political spectrum. Misinformation Review (2020)
8. Granik, M., Mesyura, V.: Fake news detection using Naive Bayes classifier. In: 2017 IEEE First Ukraine Conference on Electrical and Computer Engineering (UKRCON), pp. 900–903. IEEE (2017)
9. Horne, B., Adali, S.: This just. In: Fake news packs a lot in title, uses simpler, repetitive content in text body, more similar to satire than real news. In: Proceedings of the International AAAI Conference on Web and Social Media, vol. 11 (2017)
10. Idrees, A.M., Alsheref, F.K., ElSeddawy, A.I.: A proposed model for detecting Facebook news' credibility. Int. J. Adv. Comput. Sci. Appl. (IJACSA) **10**(7), 311–316 (2019)

11. Kovach, B., Rosenstiel, T.: The elements of journalism: what newspeople should know and the public should expect. Three Rivers Press (CA) (2014)
12. Lotan, G.: Networked audiences: attention and data-informed. The New Ethics of Journalism: Principles for the 21st Century, pp. 105–122 (2014)
13. Lundberg, S.M., et al.: From local explanations to global understanding with explainable AI for trees. Nat. Mach. Intell. **2**(1), 56–67 (2020)
14. Mahyoob, M., Al-Garaady, J., Alrahaili, M.: Linguistic-based detection of fake news in social media. Forthcom. Int. J. Engl. Linguist. **11**(1) (2020)
15. Marquardt, D.: Linguistic indicators in the identification of fake news. Mediatization Stud. **3**, 95–114 (2019)
16. Marwick A., Kuo R., C.S.J., Weigel, M.: Critical disinformation studies: a syllabus (2021)
17. Mohammad, S.: Obtaining reliable human ratings of valence, arousal, and dominance for 20,000 English words. In: Proceedings of the 56th Annual Meeting of the Association for Computational Linguistics (volume 1: Long Papers), pp. 174–184 (2018)
18. Mohammad, S.M.: Word affect intensities. arXiv preprint arXiv:1704.08798 (2017)
19. Olivieri, A., Shabani, S., Sokhn, M., Cudré-Mauroux, P.: Creating task-generic features for fake news detection. In: Proceedings of the 52nd Hawaii International Conference on System Sciences (2019)
20. Pérez-Rosas, V., Kleinberg, B., Lefevre, A., Mihalcea, R.: Automatic detection of fake news. arXiv preprint arXiv:1708.07104 (2017)
21. Plutchik, R.: A general psychoevolutionary theory of emotion. In: Theories of Emotion, pp. 3–33. Elsevier (1980)
22. Rashkin, H., Choi, E., Jang, J.Y., Volkova, S., Choi, Y.: Truth of varying shades: analyzing language in fake news and political fact-checking. In: Proceedings of the 2017 Conference on Empirical Methods in Natural Language Processing, pp. 2931–2937 (2017)
23. Reinemann, C., Stanyer, J., Scherr, S., Legnante, G.: Hard and soft news: A review of concepts, operationalizations and key findings. Journalism **13**(2), 221–239 (2012)
24. Reis, J.C., Correia, A., Murai, F., Veloso, A., Benevenuto, F.: Supervised learning for fake news detection. IEEE Intell. Syst. **34**(2), 76–81 (2019)
25. Rubin, V.L., Conroy, N., Chen, Y., Cornwell, S.: Fake news or truth? Using satirical cues to detect potentially misleading news. In: Proceedings of the Second Workshop on Computational Approaches to Deception Detection, pp. 7–17 (2016)
26. Russell, J.A.: Core affect and the psychological construction of emotion. Psychol. Rev. **110**(1), 145 (2003)
27. Shao, C., Ciampaglia, G.L., Varol, O., Flammini, A., Menczer, F.: The spread of fake news by social bots, vol. 96, p. 104. arXiv preprint arXiv:1707.07592 (2017)
28. Shouse, E.: Feeling, emotion, affect. M/c J. **8**(6) (2005)
29. Shu, K., Mahudeswaran, D., Wang, S., Lee, D., Liu, H.: Fakenewsnet: a data repository with news content, social context, and spatiotemporal information for studying fake news on social media. Big Data **8**(3), 171–188 (2020)
30. Shu, K., Sliva, A., Wang, S., Tang, J., Liu, H.: Fake news detection on social media: a data mining perspective. ACM SIGKDD Explor. Newsl. **19**(1), 22–36 (2017)
31. Tacchini, E., Ballarin, G., Della Vedova, M.L., Moret, S., de Alfaro, L.: Some like it hoax: automated fake news detection in social networks. arXiv preprint arXiv:1704.07506 (2017)
32. Tandoc, E.C., Jr., Lim, Z.W., Ling, R.: Defining "fake news" a typology of scholarly definitions. Digit. Journal. **6**(2), 137–153 (2018)

33. Tromble, R.: The (MIS) informed citizen: indicators for examining the quality of online news. Available at SSRN 3374237 (2019)
34. Wang, W.Y.: "liar, liar pants on fire": a new benchmark dataset for fake news detection. arXiv preprint arXiv:1705.00648 (2017)
35. Wilson, T., Wiebe, J., Hoffmann, P.: Recognizing contextual polarity in phrase-level sentiment analysis. In: Proceedings of Human Language Technology Conference and Conference on Empirical Methods in Natural Language Processing, pp. 347–354 (2005)

Author Index

Printed in the United States
by Baker & Taylor Publisher Services